TAKING
CHARGE

Teenagers Talk about Life & Physical Disabilities

▼ *Kay H. Kriegsman, Ph.D.*

▼ *Elinor L. Zaslow, M.A.*

▼ *Jennifer D'Zmura-Rechsteiner, M.A.*

WOODBINE HOUSE ▼ 1992

Library of Congress Cataloging-in-Publication Data

Kriegsman, Kay Harris.
    Taking charge : teenagers talk about life and physical disabilities /
Kay Harris Kriegsman, Elinor L. Zaslow, Jennifer D'Zmura-Rechsteiner.
        p. cm.
    Includes bibliographical references and index.
    Summary: Discusses such topics as independence, self-esteem, relationships,
and sexuality from the perspective of teenagers with various physical disabilities.
    ISBN 0–933149–46–8 : $14.95
    1. Physically handicapped teenagers—United States—Attitudes—Juvenile
literature. [1. Physically handicapped. 2. Youth—Attitudes.] I. Zaslow, Elinor L.
II. D'Zmura-Rechsteiner, Jennifer. III. Title.
HV888.5.K75 1992
362.4'0835—dc20   92–28253
                                                                   CIP
                                                                    AC

Manufactured in the United States of America

10 9 8 7 6 5 4 3 2 1

This book is dedicated to . . .

JOHN

APRIL

GLEN

TIFFANY

TIM

ALYSSA

EDWARD

TIMEKA

SAM

JUNE

MYLA

ART

NICOLE

AL

TINA

*. . . who shared their dreams, everyday worries, ways of coping,
and thoughts about life and living.*

TABLE OF CONTENTS

▼ ▼ ▼ ▼ ▼ ▼ ▼ ▼ ▼ ▼ ▼

i

PART THREE: How Can You Get Where You Want to Go?

APPENDIX

ACKNOWLEDGEMENTS

▼ ▼ ▼ ▼ ▼ ▼ ▼ ▼ ▼ ▼ ▼ ▼

We three have felt privileged to team-write *Taking Charge: Teenagers Talk about Life and Physical Disabilities*. We have shared many bags of microwavable popcorn, run through reams of computer paper, and met most of our deadlines! We have worked through the birthing, first steps, and maturation of this book, which in the end has taken its own unique form.

That unique form was contributed by the young people who willingly participated. Our debt is great to the fifteen teenagers who gave the treasure of their time and wisdom garnered from lifetimes of experience. We thank you!

Our appreciation also to our editor, Susan Stokes, who took our disparate styles of expression and wove them into one fabric. Her calm and confidence in the project were always evident. We also recognize the commitment of the Woodbine House team, led by publisher Irv Shapell, to projects that make a difference. . . . And to Sally Weiss of United Cerebral Palsy who first matched us with this project.

No one member of the family ever gives alone. So we thank our families for their support in encouraging, running off duplicate copies, taking phone calls, giving feedback, and freeing us up for our weekend writing confabs. Our Family Honor Roll includes Marc Rechsteiner; Milt Zaslow; and Will, Bill, and Katie Kriegsman!

Having survived the teen years with physical disabilities, Jennifer and Kay also wish to thank the D'Zmura and Harris families for allowing them to take charge.

FOREWORD
By Leslie Milk

▼   ▼   ▼   ▼   ▼   ▼   ▼

When I was growing up, a teenager with a paralyzed arm, I thought that mine was a unique kind of misery. Surely no one had ever survived the humiliation of not being asked to dance—or worse, being asked for a slow dance and not being able to put my arm on his shoulder. The anguish of skipping pool parties because it's harder to hide a handicap in a bathing suit. The hours spent worrying in advance about every unlikely embarrassment—what if somebody pushed me into the pool and I couldn't pull myself out, what if I dropped all my books because I didn't want anyone to know I couldn't carry them, what if. . . .

Now that I have been the mother of teenagers, both of whom had no obvious disability, I realize how much of my misery was and is universal. Adolescence is the ultimate disability. All teenagers hate their hands or their hair, feel stupid and awkward, and are certain that their tiny flaws and foibles are the only things others see about them.

So to be a teenager coping with adolescence and a disability is to be doubly disabled. To be different when every adolescent instinct begs for sameness, is to be denied the protective coloration that helps other kids endure the teen years, the mean years.

Taking Charge: Teenagers Talk about Life and Physical Disabilities is a book by people who have been there and teenagers who are living through it today. It pulls no punches—acknowledging that the world still puts obstacles in the paths of people with disabilities, both literally and figuratively. It offers no easy answers—the person with the disability is probably going to have to work to explain the obstacle, work to have it removed, and make the non-disabled feel good about it, all at the same time.

What *Taking Charge* offers are strategies for handling the tough issues—from siblings to sexuality, from over-protective parents to staring strangers. It is filled with the can-do spirit to help teenagers with disabilities take positive steps toward independence and begin to discover their strengths. They are already world-class experts on their weaknesses.

But for me the greatest strength of this book is the interviews with young people with disabilities. Their honesty and their courage is contagious. I found myself nodding in agreement on almost every page as they described their frustration at needing extraordinary effort to do ordinary things. The unending exasperation at not being able to do simple tasks. And the inner resources they summon to persevere anyway.

Taking Charge helps teenagers with disabilities define themselves rather than continue to be defined by their disabilities. As one young woman named June puts it: "I have cerebral palsy. I know I have some limitations, but in my mind I say I can do anything."

Me too, June. Me too.

INTRODUCTION

▼ ▼ ▼ ▼ ▼ ▼ ▼ ▼ ▼

The world is changing. It is changing for *you*. There are so many new choices—choices not available even a few years ago. This makes it an exciting time to be a person who happens to have a disability.

How is the world changing, you ask? Here are a few ways:

There are more people with disabilities on TV: on the soaps, in commercials, and on other TV shows. People using crutches or wheelchairs are models in clothing catalogs for big department stores. This is pretty important because TV and catalogs usually mirror what is happening—and what is accepted—in everyday life.

Employers are hiring more people with disabilities. They are learning that people like you have lots of abilities to offer. There is also a powerful new law, the Americans with Disabilities Act, to back up your rights to work.

Electric wheelchairs, communication devices, computer aids, and other inventions are making it possible to be more independent. It is easier to get places because there are curb cuts, ramps, elevators, and wheelchair-accessible bathrooms. You can be *in* the world, not just watching it turn.

People are beginning to understand that a disability is just one part of a person—that people are not their disabilities. That's important because they can then see what abilities someone has. They can see you as an individual.

BUT—We all know that you still have to face some problems, such as:

- Dealing with the physical reality of your disability.
- Owning your feelings—recognizing them, not denying them—about being a teenager with a disability.
- Understanding the ways others feel about your disability.
- Being a teenager . . . who also is a person with a disability.

The trick: Balance the ups and downs. That's what this book is all about. It is for you. It is not based on what some doctor or teacher or neighbor thinks is good for you. It's by and about some recent teens and some present teens who struggled with or are struggling with the dilemmas and challenges you are dealing with. They are figuring out ways to deal with these problems. They are trying creative approaches. They are making decisions about how they want to live their lives. They are trying to make their decisions and dreams become reality.

The people interviewed for this book ranged from just barely into their teens to almost out of them. Some have complete families, some don't. They are of different colors and backgrounds and circumstances. They have the full span of physical disabilities and many have additional problems with vision, hearing, speech, learning, or seizures. All are intelligent people who were willing to put up with several hours of interviewing. Some of them preferred not to answer certain questions. Each one selected a pseudonym. These are not their real names, but these are their real words.

This book is divided into three major sections. The first section is about who you are and how it feels to be you. The second part is about how you relate to other people, and how they relate to you. The last section is about how you can become as independent as possible.

Dividing the sections are three profiles of young adults with physical disabilities who have successfully come through the teenage years.

An appendix gives expert information on legal, architectural, technological, engineering, and medical developments that affect people with physical disabilities.

This is not a Pollyanna book. It is not easy to handle a wheelchair, walk with crutches or canes, move spastically, speak unclearly, limp, depend on other people a lot, sometimes live with pain. You have to be honest. You need to face your feelings. But having investigated your feelings and perhaps gotten help with them, you are ready to move beyond.

Key   You can't ignore your disability but you can't let it limit you either.

On to the questions and answers of the teenagers and young adults with disabilities we interviewed. We hope their ideas and creative solutions will give you some ways to start moving toward your dreams. We hope they will help you TAKE CHARGE!

THE TEENAGERS

▼ ▼ ▼ ▼ ▼ ▼ ▼ ▼ ▼

John is 16 and in the ninth grade. This is his first year in his home school—that is, the school where students in his neighborhood attend classes. He has cerebral palsy and uses crutches or an electric wheelchair. He also has a speech impairment and a hearing disability, and uses hearing aids in both ears.

April is 19 and is a high school graduate. She takes vocational training and works part-time for a telecommunications exchange for the deaf. She has spina bifida, walks unaided for short distances, and uses crutches or a wheelchair for longer distances.

Glen, 15, is a sophomore in high school who has osteogenesis imperfecta. He wears leg braces and sometimes uses crutches or a wheelchair.

Tiffany is 17 and is a junior in a high school program for students with orthopedic disabilities. She has cerebral palsy and walks without aids. Because she has a speech disability, she uses a speaking device and signs to communicate.

Tim is 15. He is a junior in high school. He has muscular dystrophy and uses electric and manual wheelchairs.

Alyssa is 18 and a senior in high school. She spends a half day in a work/study program and a half day in academic courses. She has osteogenesis imperfecta and uses one crutch to walk—two if walking a long distance.

Edward is 18. He is a freshman in college. He has muscular dystrophy and uses a wheelchair.

Timeka, 18, is a senior in high school. She has spina bifida and uses a wheelchair.

Sam is 15. He is a high school freshman who has cerebral palsy. He uses a walker or a wheelchair in different situations. He also has limited vision, epilepsy, and a learning disability.

June is 17, a senior in a boarding high school. She has cerebral palsy and walks without assistance.

Myla is 14. She is an eighth grader. She has spina bifida and uses crutches and braces to walk.

Art, 19, is a high school graduate. He has spina bifida and uses a wheelchair.

Nicole is a 14–year-old ninth grader who is attending her home high school for the first time. She has cerebral palsy and uses an electric wheelchair.

Al is 19. He is a high school graduate. He has spina bifida and uses a walker and a wheelchair.

Tina is 12, and an eighth grader in a program for students with orthopedic disabilities. She has muscular dystrophy and uses an electric wheelchair. She also has a Canine Companion.

WALTER'S STORY

▼ *Walter Slater, 22, doesn't like people to tell him "no." Although his cerebral palsy affects his speech and right arm motion, he walks unaided. He says, "Just give me a chance, and I'll prove my ability."*

Recently Walter proved his ability by learning to drive. He says, "I got my driver's license last June and everyone was so surprised. No one thought I could do it, but I did." He has also learned to operate a front loader machine at the construction site where his brother-in-law, George Bishop, works. And in 1987, he graduated from high school.

In fact, Walter has made a lifelong habit of challenging others' expectations. He recalls that when he was twelve he scared one of his brothers to death when he announced he had learned to ride a bike. Later on, when somebody stole his bike, he tried hard to recover it on his own. When Walter found out who had taken his bike, he confronted him. Against his better judgment, he was suddenly in a fist fight with the neighborhood bully. Walter didn't get his bike back, but that day was very important for him. He explains, "People always think that people with disabilities never get in trouble. I was not proud of the fact I was in a fight, but I think I showed the kids in my area that I am just like everyone else."

Not only do the neighborhood kids now accept Walter, but they also come to him to fix their bikes. And, Walter notes, "Once people get to know me, they forget I am handicapped."

One reason Walter has never really let his disability become a handicap is because of his family—his parents, five brothers, and seven sisters. He says, "Basically, my family treated me like a 'normal' person. My family always said, 'Do it yourself.' I never wanted or received any special favors or treatment." About the only complaint he has about his disability is that the communication difficulties he encounters can be frustrating.

Walter's claims are backed up by George Bishop, who sometimes serves as Walter's interpreter and appears to be his best friend. "Walter has always been a normal part of the family," George agrees. "He fought and played with his brothers and sisters. They all took care of each other. I

have a lot of respect for Walter. He wasn't allowed to get away with anything."

At present, Walter lives at home with his mom and dad, as well as three sisters and one brother. But he hopes to increase his independence soon—specifically, by finding a job that will pay him enough to live comfortably.

Until recently, Walter divided his time between part-time paid work and part-time volunteer work. Walter's paid job was at an auto repair shop, where he helped clean up and learned to repair cars. His volunteer job was with an organization called Youth for Understanding, where he mailed out brochures to people interested in their student-exchange program. Walter says this volunteer work was "something to do and good experience." But he warns that people with disabilities need to be choosy about the volunteer work they accept. In high school, for instance, he worked for a computer company, doing volunteer work that he felt he should have been paid for. He says, "Sometimes

people take advantage of the handicapped. You have to not be afraid to take a stand." For Walter, taking a stand meant quitting his volunteer job and taking a paying job with a company that made microfilm. Presently, Walter works full time for a major hotel chain, in the housekeeping department.

In his free time, Walter keeps busy with his hobbies—fishing, bike racing, and "tearing down car engines in order to find a problem." Every Friday night he works out at a gym that lets people with disabilities in for free. When he finishes, he says, "I help out others who may be in

a wheelchair and need help with the weights. I hate sitting around with nothing to do."

When asked what words of advice he has for other young people with disabilities, Walter offers a handful: "Stop making excuses for yourself. Be persistent—don't think about what other people say. If you get the chance to do something, do it! Don't miss the chance. Don't wait for a handout—earn it yourself. Make something happen for yourself."

PART 1

▼

WHO ARE YOU?

    This first section deals with how it feels to be a teenager with a physical disability. A number of different issues are touched on, including self-image, sexuality, making a good impression, dealing with unwanted attention, and coping with frustration and depression.

    Your views on these subjects may be similar to some expressed here, or they may be completely different. Obviously, teenagers with disabilities have just as many ways of looking at themselves as other teenagers. Understanding exactly who *you* are happens gradually. It's a complicated process involving good and bad experiences and good and bad choices, as well as opportunity, determination, and luck. The goal is to feel comfortable with who you are now so you can make the choices and have the experiences that will enable you to live the life you want to live in the future.

    Reading what other teenagers have to say in this section about their identities may help guide you to a better understanding of your own identity. Ideally, you will also find some new strategies for coping with your feelings and concerns.

CHAPTER 1

JUST WHO DO YOU THINK YOU ARE?

▼ ▼ ▼ ▼ ▼ ▼ ▼ ▼ ▼

To get everyone thinking about who they are—or at least, who they *think* they are—we asked:

How would you describe yourself?

John: I'm very shy, but I like physical challenge. I'm a hard worker once I put my mind to it. Also, I'm a little bit crazy—like I do weird stuff and try to make people laugh. I like playing video games and reading adventure, mystery, and supernatural stories. I just started drawing characters for a new video game I'm creating.

April: I'm friendly and caring, a good listener, out-going, easy to talk to. I'm short—a very short person for my age—and I'm cute. Swimming, wheelchair sports, listening to the radio and tapes, going to the mall, and reading are my hobbies. I like any kind of book except mysteries, and I read *Teen Beat* magazine.

Glen: I'm creative and a leader. When the teacher has us work in a group, I'm the one who says "Let's do *this*." I love animals: a lizard, five fish, and a cat are my pets now, but I want an iguana. I enjoy read-ing, especially science fiction, and throwing a ball around with friends.

Tiffany: I'm a happy person. I like to have fun, but I'm also pretty serious. I listen to books on tape and am into art. I won first prize in a drawing competi-tion.

Tim: I'm a nice guy, funny, and I like to have a good time. But I have a serious side, too: I want to be helpful. My hobbies are reading, especially about nature and the outdoors, swimming, going to the mall, listening to the radio, and playing video games and my electric keyboard.

Alyssa: I'm outgoing and fun to be with. I listen to everyone's problems. They can trust me. I used to draw a lot but don't have time now. I like to listen to music: heavy metal like Metallica and mellower sounds like Poison, and I read mysteries and horror stories.

Edward: I'm easygoing. I don't worry about stuff even if it's hard. I'm shy, but if people are nice to me I'm friendly. My hobbies are drawing cartoon characters, watching TV, especially sports, using a computer, and listening to rock and roll and jazz. If I see a good movie I like to read the book it was based on.

Timeka: I'm outgoing up to a point. I like to be around people, and I'm the center of attention a lot. Drawing, swimming, phoning, going out, and watching TV are my hobbies.

Sam: I'm very calm, very settled, very well-planned. I enjoy radio broadcasting (we have a system in our house) and constructing with blocks. I read large-print books and just finished the Hardy Boys series.

June: I'm outgoing, quite self-assured, and I enjoy meeting people. I'm aware of how far I've come, where I am now, and have definite goals about where I want to go. My hobbies are shopping, riding a bike, and jogging. I read *Seventeen* and *Vogue* magazines.

Myla: A child likes to live her life like everybody else does. I have some problems, so I have to get around them. I like listening to music and making jewelry, particularly earrings and bracelets, using wire, leather, and suede mostly. I don't care much for reading. I enjoy aerobics class in school. Sometimes I speak to groups on genetics and disabilities.

Art: I'm cheerful, outgoing, fun to be around. I'm a collector—of baseball and football cards, stamps and coins, and tennis balls.

Nicole: I try to be patient and not too demanding. I'm nice to others. I don't try to get everything I want; I'm not spoiled, and I don't want to be. Writing stories, listening to music—Christian music and light rock—and baking and cooking are my hobbies. I like adventure, mystery, and "Choose Your Own" books.

Al: I'm cute, mature, athletic, strong, outgoing, and intelligent. I like talking on the phone, going out to eat, playing wheelchair tennis, going handicapped skiing, and traveling. I read the sports section of the paper sometimes.

Tina: I'm pretty happy. I'm hard working and I set goals for myself. I'm pretty competitive and determined. I like doing small tasks with my hands: crocheting and cross-stitching, drawing and painting, and filing papers. The books I like are the "Babysitter" series, romances, and mysteries.

Although these teenagers all have physical limitations, you probably couldn't guess it from reading most of their descriptions of themselves. As with any group of teenagers, they have a wide range of personalities, interests, and outlooks. True, their disabilities have shaped who they are and what they do to some extent. None of them are involved in contact sports, for example. And most of them like to read, work with computers, or do other sit-down activities. But these folks don't see their physical disabilities as the deciding factor in who they are—or who they are becoming.

Think about how you would describe yourself. Is the first thing that springs to mind that you are a disabled teenager? Or do you think of yourself more as a well-rounded person who just happens to have a dis-

ability? Maybe the distinction doesn't seem all that important to you. But how you answer the question does tell you where you are putting the emphasis.

Is that man primarily:

- a dentist
- a Mormon
- a demanding father
- a jogger?

Is that girl primarily:

- an African-American
- a whiz at math
- a swimmer
- someone who teases her brothers?

Are you primarily:

- a cheerful kid
- a disabled person
- an artist
- a poet
- an angry or pitiful kid
- an overweight person
- class clown
- a bookworm
- a flirt
- . . . or what?

It would probably not be possible, or even desirable, to try to over-look the hard fact that you have a disability. But you also have many other characteristics. You are not *just* your disability. You have multiple facets, and they are developing and changing—and sometimes quite con-fusing—during this stage of life. Defining and refining tastes and preferences, interests, talents, likes and dislikes are all parts of becoming an adult. And they are all parts of *you*.

At the moment, you may or may not be able to see yourself as separate from your disability. But whether you can or not, you know it's impossible to divorce yourself from it completely. Every day you live with your disability and the challenges it brings to your life. Just as these teenagers do, you probably have strong feelings about what it means to have a disability. We asked them:

How do you describe your disability?

John: It's a very tough challenge. Some people can make it and some can't. It depends on your attitude and how you've been raised.

April: The muscles are weak in my legs and it's physically hard to get around sometimes.

Glen: O.I. isn't as crippling as most. Seeing other handicapped people makes me realize I'm lucky to have this disease. I can walk to a certain extent. I'm not mentally handicapped. My disease has gotten better over my lifetime. When explaining O.I., I say it is a disease affecting the connective tissue of my body. Basically, it makes my bones brittle. I break my bones a lot, especially the ones in my legs.

Tiffany: I'm not able to talk, and sometimes I have to use a crutch in my right hand to walk in crowds.

Tim: I feel useless. I can't get up or play sports. I feel guilty because it's like a punishment.

Alyssa: It's brittle-bone disease.

Edward: It worsens all the time. I have to take it as it comes. I don't know what will happen in a year.

Timeka: I'm paralyzed from the waist down, but I have some feeling. I need help with my braces and crutches; everything else I can usually do.

Sam: My disability is sometimes hard, sometimes easy. It's in the middle.

June: When discussing my cerebral palsy, I say it won't get worse and it won't improve. It impairs my motor skills. It's a condition I've come to accept. The more I work, the better it'll be for my character.

Myla: My disability is tough to deal with. I have to use crutches and braces, and I have to use a catheter to go to the bathroom. I hate it! And I can't braid my own hair.

Art: I don't know—I don't think of myself as having a disability.

Nicole: If someone appears to be curious about my disability or the subject comes up, I will explain my disability as a part of my life. If I described it to a child, I'd say that the part of the brain that's supposed to tell my legs to walk isn't working well. If I were telling an adult, I'd say that the cerebellum controlling my leg muscles was hurt when I was a baby because I was twelve weeks premature.

Al: When I meet people for the first time, I explain that I have a birth defect called spina bifida that affects my limbs. I do not tell others about my learning disability. It doesn't show, so why should I explain it? I feel lucky because there are others who have a more severe form of the same disability. I can do more things and I can do them easier. The teachers in my elementary school taught us that we are "handicapable."

Tina: I tell strangers that I have muscular dystrophy, and I am the same as anybody else but I am very weak . . . and you cannot hurt me. It's not contagious. I can't walk and I have a hard time opening doors.

If you read between the lines, you can see that these teenagers have a variety of attitudes toward their disabilities: acceptance, denial, optimism, depression, practicality, idealism. How *you* look at *your* disability depends on a lot of factors. Some factors are beyond your control. These include the nature and extent of your disability; perhaps your ability to afford expensive technology that can help you; and other considerations that have to do with where you live, who you live with, and what opportunities are available.

But other factors are very much under your control. These include:

- your coping skills and your attitudes;
- your knowledge of your disability and how you can mini-mize its effects on your life; and
- your willingness to try new things.

You might be able to concentrate more of your attention on these aspects of being you—the ones you do have control over.

To help you learn to control those aspects of your life that you can, the next section focuses on coping skills. And the Appendix includes in-formation designed to help you increase your knowledge of various dis-ability issues. As for discovering new interests, you may not need any guidance. But if you do, here are some suggestions:

Maybe, like John, you can develop your skills as a comedian; or like Alyssa, be a thoughtful listener people like to confide in. You might also pursue an interest in some special subject: fossilized plants or the mechanics of flight or fabric design or jazz. Delving into some field you find stimulating gives you focus and makes you interesting to yourself and to others. You will find organizations, clubs, and groups of people who have the same interests. Your involvement and enjoyment of life grow, and so do your self-esteem and confidence.

Can you volunteer some of your time to help others? Non-profit charitable organizations always need help with phoning, putting together newsletters, fund-raising, and sending thank-you notes to con-tributors. You might want to help an organization devoted to your par-ticular disability, or one that has nothing at all to do with it.

Most politicians got their start stuffing envelopes or answering phones for a local candidate. You can get involved in a political cam-paign in your area, and maybe influence policies that affect people with disabilities, or the environment, or whatever you care about.

Problem If you volunteer, beware of "tokenism." As Walter sug-gests (page 4), be sure that you are given real work to do, and are not just there to show the world how tolerant that organization is of people with disabilities. Insist that your real talents be recognized and used. For example, if you have a flair for writing, ask if you can sometimes write for the newsletter instead of spending all your time typing other people's work.

Idea   If you don't have a special interest, you could ask other
people how they got interested in something they do. You
may find that an interest was triggered by overhearing
someone talking, seeing something on TV, reading, going
to a meeting or lecture, joining a school club, noticing a
need, wondering how something works, trying out for a
play, visiting a museum, making a new acquaintance.
Sometimes interests are developed deliberately, but more
often they grow quite by accident.

CHAPTER 2

COPING WITH YOUR EMOTIONS

▼ ▼ ▼ ▼ ▼ ▼ ▼ ▼ ▼ ▼ ▼ ▼ ▼ ▼ ▼

Everybody's life is full of minor and major annoyances. Some of the daily stresses and problems *you* face may be related to having a disability, while others may not. In either case, identifying the problem is usually the first step in being able to cope with it. To find out what kinds of things often bother teenagers with physical disabilities, we asked:

What bothers you most about having a disability?

John: Not doing what other people take for granted. I wanted to be on the basketball team, but I can't because of my legs. But I may be the assistant manager of the team.

April: Not being able to do normal things, like driving. And my seizures!

Glen: Seeing people running around. When I think about those things I feel frustrated, but usually it doesn't bother me.

There are stairs in our school cafeteria separating the upper and lower levels. I can get to the upper part, but to get to the lower level I have to go outside and go around part of the school to a different door. I couldn't believe a school only two years old would have steps in the cafeteria!

An English assignment was to write a letter of complaint. I wrote about the cafeteria situation and sent my letter to the Superintendent of Schools. The response I got was that the cafeteria met the "specs" for accessibility. But I don't think that's right. "Accessible" should mean I can get to *all* parts, not just some.

Tiffany: I don't like people staring at me because of my disability.

Tim: Not being able to walk.

Alyssa: I can't reach things up high. I can't carry some things. I can't walk long distances without tiring.

Edward: Not knowing what will happen with my disability; not being able to do some things, like reach things. I want to be more independent, and I can't.

Timeka: Not being able to go places like others my age. I don't live where my friends do, and taking my wheelchair is difficult.

Sam: Seizures—they're frightening. There's no warning and they last different amounts of time. Now that I'm in high school I can go to the guidance counselor when I have a seizure, and my mother doesn't have to leave work.

June: Having to come to terms with it; having to face my limitations and still keep my self-esteem up.

Myla: I can't do the things I want to do the way I want to do them.

Art: Not being able to play the sports I want to; for example, football.

Nicole: When people make fun of me and laugh at me. I'm learning to deal with it more maturely.

Al: Not being able to do some things with the rest of my family, such as getting into inaccessible places when we're on a trip.

Tina: When I can't do things with friends, like running—and not being as strong.

Certainly these folks have hit on most of the major frustrations that confront young people with physical disabilities. They're bothered by not being able to participate fully or at all in activities that cannot be adapted for someone with physical limitations. John wants to play basketball and can't; Art wants to play football and can't; Timeka, Al, and Tina would like to go some places that others go, and can't. Some have worries about medical issues: pain, seizures, upcoming surgeries, the possibility that time may be running out.

They are also concerned about being more dependent on others than they'd like to be. Like April, you may feel frustrated that you can't drive, or you may be depressed that you can't take care of your own bathroom needs, or make your speech clear, or wear ordinary shoes. All these things are especially frustrating when what you really want is to be like other people your age, and to be independent.

There is no one right way to cope with your frustrations about having a disability. But here are some ways the teenagers consulted for this book deal with their anger, frustration, and depression. We asked them:

How do you feel most of the time?

What if you are angry or depressed?

John: I'm usually calm and cool, but sometimes frustrated and sometimes scared. When I'm frustrated I may cry—sometimes I want to scream. When I get angry I want to do something physical, like throw something, maybe hit the wall. But it's rare for me to feel depressed.

April: Usually I'm happy and satisfied, but I feel sad once in awhile. If I feel frustrated I just go in my room and have time by myself. If I felt angry, I'd probably stay in my room longer.

Glen: Most of the time I feel good, but of course not always. When I'm frustrated I keep working at the problem until I can do better, or I find a way to work around it. When I feel depressed I talk to friends, especially girls; they're more sympathetic. I don't talk to my parents when I'm feeling depressed—I don't know why. Time defuses anger.

Tiffany: Usually I'm happy and full of fun, but sometimes I'm serious and sometimes scared. Once in awhile I feel both angry and frustrated.

Tim: I feel frustrated in school and bored most of the time. When I'm frustrated I try to think about the good things in life. When I'm angry I may yell or destroy things. I try to forget it by going outside to get away from the situation.

Alyssa: Mostly I feel fine, but I always feel tired. If I'm frustrated about something I'll turn the radio on really loud. If I'm angry it depends on who I'm mad at: if it's my parents, I try to ignore it; if it's my boyfriend, I try to hide it—I won't let him know I'm mad. If I feel depressed I may stay in my room by myself, or I may talk to friends. I don't talk to my parents about it; I don't feel it's any of their business.

Edward: Usually I feel all right—not great, but OK, and different depending on the time of day—it changes all the time. Sometimes I get frustrated, but I guess that's normal. If I do feel frustrated I just go into my room, listen to the radio, stare at the wall, and try to figure out why I'm so frustrated. I try not to let it go so far that I feel depressed, though I may feel sad.

Timeka: I feel mostly happy. If I do feel frustrated or angry I may sit down and try to work out the problem by myself, or I may talk to someone close to me and even ask for advice.

Sam: At school I often feel depressed, but at home I usually feel happy. When I feel frustrated I go to my room and listen to Talking Books. When I'm angry I may clam up and not talk for four or five days, and then my parents find out. I have a secret spot outside where I go to cool off. Only my brother and one friend know where that secret spot is.

June: I'm usually happy. When I feel frustrated I look at the things I have done and try not to dwell on the things I can't do. When I'm angry I can lose my temper, though. If I ever feel depressed I turn to my family. They can tell me their feelings, so I see I'm not the only one who has felt that way.

Myla: It's a hard life. I feel angry and tired lots of times, sometimes sad, frustrated all the time. Yet I'm almost always satisfied and lively. When I feel frustrated I just keep trying to do what I'm doing. If I feel depressed or angry I usually listen to music or watch TV. My frustration usually comes from trying to do the things my friends do, even though I *know* I can't.

Art: Calm and sincere are the words that describe how I feel most of the time. If I feel frustrated I sit back and try to relax myself. If I feel a little depressed I may read a book, watch TV, or listen to the radio.

Nicole: Most of the time I feel happy and satisfied, because I'm not interested in feeling sorry for myself. If I feel frustrated I may cry—when the elevator at school got stuck, for example. If I feel angry I sometimes write my feelings down on paper and keep it. Later I'll read it over and maybe learn from the feelings I had. If I feel depressed, it depends on whether it's because of something that happened or because of physical pain. If it's physical I try to get relief and probably go to the doctor.

One of my best friends passed away recently. I went to the body viewing and to the funeral. I sent flowers to her parents and wrote them a letter. I wrote a story about this friend. At school we had a grief workshop and we all could cry. All of these things helped, but I'm still depressed about it.

Al: I feel good most of the time. If I ever do feel frustrated or angry or depressed I can usually get over it by talking to different friends on the phone.

Tina: I'm lively, happy, active, and energetic. When I'm angry at home I go in my room, shut the door, and turn on the radio. When I'm angry at school I may take it out on the teacher or assistant.

Different ways of handling feelings are appropriate for different people, obviously. Spending time alone works best for some; others want to talk feelings over with family or friends. Some express feelings by crying, screaming, throwing things, writing down what they feel, or trying to think of something positive. How you deal with feelings helps to define your individual personality.

Once you have calmed down enough to think rationally, it may help to do as Nicole suggests. That is, try to identify exactly what is bothering you and then take constructive action. For example, if you're in more physical pain than usual, it makes sense to see your doctor. If someone has done something to make you angry, talk to them. Tell them why you are mad and see if you can work out a way to prevent similar problems in the future.

Let's say that you were left out of an activity or not invited to an event you really wanted to attend. Try to find out, as calmly as you can, why this happened. Did someone think that your disability would prevent you from taking part? Or did something you did—or did not do—contribute to the problem? For example, did you act as if you wouldn't be interested? Let people know that you wanted to be included and that you hope to be included next time. Most "slights" are unintentional, not deliberate. Sulking and brooding about them won't fix them. But taking decisive steps to make yourself feel better is a vital part of taking control of your life. See Part 2 for more suggestions about resolving conflicts with others.

It may be hard to tell if you are doing a fairly good job of handling your feelings. Everybody's emotions are like yo-yos at times. But if you feel negative almost all the time, are deeply depressed, or feel totally isolated, you need to get some help. Signs that you may need help with coping include:

- trouble falling or staying asleep
- sleeping more than usual
- not feeling like eating, or wanting to eat all the time
- not caring how you look
- not wanting to be with people
- difficulty concentrating
- not caring for activities you usually enjoy

Even if you think that no one could possibly understand, you really have to find someone who will at least try, and who may be able to help you. Perhaps it will be a school counselor, a teacher, a therapist, a support group, an uncle, a psychologist, a neighbor, a minister, a nurse. If one is not helpful, try another one.

It may be especially useful to talk things over with another kid who is in the same boat with you—especially if you don't feel comfortable talking with an adult. Finding someone who is about your age and is coping with about the same problems could benefit you both. You may have to look for a "pen pal" or "phone pal" if no one in your area fits the bill. One of the national organizations listed at the end of this book could probably help you find a few people to choose from.

Key   No one expects you to be smiling and happy and satisfied all the time. But constantly keeping gloom and despair bottled up inside can be dangerous. Looking for help is one sign of health.

CHAPTER 3

DATING, SEXUALITY, AND MARRIAGE

▼ ▼ ▼ ▼ ▼ ▼ ▼ ▼ ▼

Thinking about relationships with the opposite sex and about what lies ahead probably occupies an important place in your mind. This is understandable, considering all the physical, mental, and emotional changes that are a part of growing up. At least occasionally, everybody worries about whether what they are feeling is "normal." Everybody also worries about whether others find them attractive. And everybody worries about doing the wrong thing on a date. Obviously, having a physical disability doesn't exempt you from these "normal" worries about sexuality, and you may also have other worries specifically related to your disability. Since learning about your sexuality is a big part of learning who you are, we asked:

What are your concerns about dating, sex, and marriage?

John: I haven't even had a date yet. Sometimes I fantasize about marriage, but I haven't really thought about it much. Sex education at school last year gave me the general information. My parents have tried to talk to me about it, but we haven't had a real discussion yet.

April: I've had a lot of dates. My parents explained about sex. I haven't thought much about marriage or children yet—I think that's ten or fifteen years ahead.

Glen: I had a date—it was a mutual thing—and we went to the movies and walked around the mall. I felt a kind of general nervousness about it, like any kid would have, but it turned out OK. I've learned most about sex from TV and movies, and a lot from my parents. I never got the Big Talk, but they answered all my questions. I have basic fears about impotence that all guys have. I have thought about marriage. All the TV shows now have people whose marriages are falling apart. I want to remain married all my life. So I have the fear of not finding the right person. I would want to have children, but I would be concerned that they might have the same disease I have, or a mental handicap.

Alyssa: I've always had boyfriends, ever since I was fifteen, and I've had five long-term boyfriends. My mom says I go out with bums, but she doesn't stop me from seeing them. I don't know if I'd ever want children; I don't have patience with kids over three or four.

June: I've been invited on dates for dinner and movies. Usually I find I don't have to be concerned about dates because I find myself with people who are understanding. I've thought about marriage and always wonder if there is something I could not do, with body posturing maybe. I would rather marry an able-bodied person, I think. But whoever I'm with will be understanding. I would like to have children, but I would worry about raising them. Younger children can be cruel, and I wouldn't want them to be teased about me.

Myla: Recently I had my first date—well, kind of; I don't know if you'd actually call it a date. I went to a girl's party at her house, and her brother asked me out to eat. I was nervous, but I didn't need to be.

It turned out to be fun. I have thought about marriage and am concerned about how much money I'd have to spend. I'm not sure I'd like to have children. My kids would probably ask me, "What's wrong? What happened?" and it would be hard for them. If I picked them up at school, their friends would ask and it would be hard for them to explain. I've learned about sex from school and my mother, but I don't feel comfortable talking to my mother about it.

Art: I think about marriage or a long-term relationship all the time and wonder if it will happen. I have never had a date.

Nicole: The school homecoming dance with a mixed group of disabled and non-disabled friends was my first date. I've given some thought to marriage but have no conclusions yet. Some of my friends have a non-disabled boy friend; that could be an interesting experience. If possible, I'd like to have children, but I wouldn't want them ever to be ashamed of me. But that's a long time away. My mom told me everything there is about sex. The sad thing is when people *aren't* told about sex and suffer the consequences the rest of their lives.

Al: I asked a girl to the senior prom at my school and she asked me to hers, so I had two dates in a row. I hadn't seen the girl for six years and I was anxious but excited. It turned out there was nothing to worry about. I felt comfortable and we had a good time. I haven't thought about marriage really. I would like to have relationships, but the women I know are too old for me or not single. I think I'd like to have children, but wonder if I can. I've never asked my doctor about it.

Tina: I've had a boyfriend but no date; my mother says I can't date until I'm sixteen. She has explained sex to me. I don't think much about marriage, but I would like to have children. I'd probably adopt at least one—maybe more, so they wouldn't be lonely.

Sex is a sensitive subject for everybody, but especially for people your age. Some did not want to answer questions about it. Like you, these people have dreams and worries, and, like you, they are concerned about physical limitations.

Al's suggestion about asking the doctor whether your disability might affect your sexual abilities is a good idea. But some people might be too embarrassed to discuss sexual matters with their doctor.

Books and articles can be helpful with some specifics. For example, in *Sex, Love, and the Physically Handicapped*, Evelyn West Ayrault writes:

Too often, sex is assumed to belong only to beautiful, young, whole people. Only when these attitudes are abolished will there be fairness for people who have cerebral palsy, spina bifida, multiple sclerosis, arthritis, and other . . . syndromes. Then and only then can emphasis be placed upon, and something be done about, finding a remedy for the mechanical difficulties. Then people will stop being clinical and start being human (page 28).

Later, Ayrault notes, ". . . the handicapped person may have to make adaptations in his sexual behavior. If he is confined to a wheelchair, wears braces, has a catheter, or walks on crutches, his sexual activity may have to be planned in a realistic way" (page 81). The author then describes some specific adaptations and adjustments that can be tried, and later states "The fundamental point is that body contact is in itself pleasurable. . . ." (page 101).*

A similar point is made by Susan Heighway in her article, "Promoting Healthy Sexual Development for Adolescents with Developmental Disabilities or Chronic Illnesses." She states, "It is important to note that society's attitudes toward those with disabilities is often more of a hindrance to an adolescent's sexual development than any limitation of the condition itself" (page 5).

---

*   *Sex, Love and the Physically Handicapped* by Evelyn West Ayrault. Copyright © 1981 by Evelyn West Ayrault. Reprinted by permission of The Continuum Publishing Company.

Decision Point

Joe thought Judy was beautiful and witty and intelligent, but her cerebral palsy seemed like a pretty big barrier. None of his friends dated girls who were in wheelchairs. As he thought about it, though, what other guys were doing didn't seem so important. He really wanted to be with Judy. So Joe and Judy started dating when she was seventeen and he was eighteen.

Joe was careful to check that the places they wanted to go were wheelchair-accessible. Once he made reservations at a dinner theater after being assured it was accessible. The theater was—but not the women's bathroom! The manager suggested that Judy use the men's bathroom, which was equipped for wheelchairs. She was horribly embarrassed!

As their relationship developed, Joe wanted to show his affection by hugging and kissing Judy, and Judy wanted that, too. But her body wouldn't cooperate. She would tighten up and become spastic. Once when Joe began to kiss her, Judy's leg started to shake. He felt rebuffed, and he worried that either he was doing something wrong, or that Judy didn't care for him as much as he cared for her. They went through a rough time.

One night after a movie, Judy finally explained to Joe that her reactions to his physical affection were just a part of her c.p. She assured Joe that she wasn't rejecting him. And she suggested a better position to be in for hugs and kisses. This honesty cleared up the problems. Being honest about her physical limitations made all the difference.

Another book, . . . *All Things Are Possible,* by Yvonne Duffy, was written by and about women with physical disabilities. It is full of specific, candid information. *Toward Intimacy,* by the Task Force on Concerns of Physically Disabled Women, contains similar information and has drawings as well. *Table Manners: A Guide to the Pelvic Examination for Disabled Women and Health Care Providers,* is an illustrated booklet written by two women with physical disabilities. It is practical and explicit.

Sexuality & Handicap: Problems of Motor Handicapped People, by Dechesne, Pons, and Schellen is a more medically oriented book, technical in style. *A Parent's Guide to Spina Bifida,* by Bloom and Seljeskog, is an

example of a book devoted to one particular disability that includes sexual concerns. Examples of issues covered include: "When talking to people with spina bifida, it is important not to limit the discussions to 'plumbing'"(page 67) and, "In fact, women . . . and men with spina bifida can have satisfying sex lives" (page 68). *Enabling Romance: A Guide to Love, Sex, and Relationships for the Disabled (and the people who care about them)*, was written by a married couple, Ken Kroll and Erica Levy Klein, one of them with a disability. It is meant for mature readers. ". . . A disability plays a relatively minor role in most relationships once the couple has decided they genuinely want to be together. . . . it is the strengths and weaknesses of the people involved—not the superficialities—that determine success" is one of their encouraging comments (page 13).

These books were all found in public libraries. Although a few are out of print, you should still be able to find them or others like them on the shelves. The articles cited came from the organizations that published them. See the Resources section at the end of the book for complete bibliographic information on these books and articles.

Organizations are another source of answers to your questions about sexual relationships. United Cerebral Palsy Associations, Inc., the Muscular Dystrophy Association, the Spina Bifida Association of America, the Osteogenesis Imperfecta Organization, Planned Parenthood, and other groups have pamphlets, books, and sometimes films that can answer questions. Addresses for these organizations are listed in the back of the book.

Questions about family planning—health and economic considerations, spacing of children, birth control decisions and methods—arise naturally with questions about sex. It is best *not* to rely on only one source for answers. You can consult with family members, doctors and nurses, clergy, people who have tried different approaches, and some of the organizations listed above. All can give you insights and guidance. But the deciding factors will, of course, be your own situation and preferences.

It is vital to be aware of your own needs and desires. It is equally necessary to consider the needs and desires of your partner. You and your partner need to be aware and honest about your concerns about sexually transmitted diseases—especially AIDS—which are a part of the modern world. You can obtain information from your school nurse, the city or county health department, or from a doctor with whom you feel comfortable.

What about heredity? Maybe you are concerned, as Glen is, that you might pass your condition on to your children. If so, it's fairly easy to find out what the chances are of that happening. Genetic counselors may be recommended by physicians, school personnel, rehabilitation staff members, clergy, or your local chapter of the March of Dimes and Birth Defects Foundation. You might also want to find a copy of *The Family Genetic Sourcebook* by Benjamin A. Pierce. This book gives clear information about the percentage chances of inheriting many genetic traits, including epilepsy, neural tube defects, osteogenesis imperfecta, and muscular dystrophy. The book also includes state-by-state listings of clinical genetic service centers and of genetic service coordinators, who can give individual consultations and guidance.

Perhaps you are not as worried about the possibility of having children with disabilities as you are about your own abilities to cope as a parent with disabilities. For instance, June, Myla, and Nicole all worry that their children might be teased or embarrassed about having a parent with disabilities. But children's attitudes and their abilities to deal with differences are learned from those around them. Surely no one is in a better position to help their children understand disabilities *and* develop skills for dealing with ill-informed people than parents who have disabilities!

Maybe—like John, Art, and Tina—you haven't had a date yet. If so, worries about children may seem premature. Perhaps you are more concerned about your attractiveness to others. Most teenagers, with and without disabilities, worry about this a lot. In fact, many aspects of sexual

Decision Point

Chrissy was taking a course on Contemporary Issues and the Family one semester. One of the discussion questions was "Do you want to have children?" Chrissy had always dreamed of having children. True, she used a wheelchair and had some strength limitations, but she had always found a way to do the things she really wanted to do. After the class discussion on the topic, Chrissy described her classmates' different points of view to her mother. Her mother listened attentively, then said, "Chrissy, I think that you should think this one through. You just don't understand the amount of work and physical stamina a baby requires. When you get married, I think it would be much wiser if you think about adopting older children who will be able to do for themselves. A baby would just be impossible for you to handle." Chrissy was stunned. Her family had never said she "couldn't do" before. She told her mother that she was sorry that she felt that way. Chrissy knew that she would be able to find ways to handle a baby by herself.

Chrissy did find creative ways to have and raise a baby in partnership with her husband, Hal. They have two young daughters and a baby boy. Chrissy does become fatigued. But the other young mothers she knows who don't have disabilities are also tired. She and Hal have spent many hours researching the kinds of baby furniture and equipment that make it easier for Chrissy to care for their children. Their home is organized so that all members of the family can use it. And Chrissy and Hal have never created a game out of running after the children. Chrissy doesn't want the children to run from her into a busy street.

maturing will be basically the same for you as for others your age. For example, eating right and getting as much regular exercise as you can will help you look your best. Other basic do's and don't's include:

- Keep yourself clean and smelling good.
- Dress appropriately.
- Set clear limits.
- Avoid provocative or suggestive looks or comments if you are not ready for the consequences.

- Protect yourself from unwanted attentions. For example, if you are in a wheelchair, wearing a short skirt may not be the best idea even if that's what's in style. You can develop your own style.

In the end, satisfying sexual relationships probably have more to do with affection, caring, trust, and security than with physical prowess. And as trite as it may sound, compassion is just as important as passion.

CHAPTER 4

WHAT'S EVERYBODY LOOKING AT?

▼   ▼   ▼   ▼   ▼   ▼   ▼   ▼

Even if *you* forget you have a disability, others always seem to be reminding you. We asked our interviewees:

How do you deal with unwanted remarks, stares, and attention?

John: Due to shyness, I do not have much experience introducing myself to strangers. I am beginning to say, "Hi, I'm John. What's your name?" If I get questions about my disability, I give strangers the basics and describe how I got it.

Alyssa: It's usually little children because they don't understand. If they're just very small, sweet children, I don't mind. If they are irritating kids I will be rude. I stare, or say, "Excuse me, is there a problem?" Friends say I shouldn't talk like that, but I don't care, because I think those kids' mothers should teach them manners.

Edward: I don't mind answering questions. But I wait to be asked. If a stranger asks me to describe my disability, I explain how muscular dystrophy gets worse.

One day I asked the lady in the cafeteria to take money from my wallet to pay for my lunch. She got all mad. I felt bad for her. She doesn't know how to feel about other people. Sometimes I feel I should say something in a situation like that, but I don't. I just give them the cold shoulder.

Timeka: Sometimes little kids stare. I don't mind; they are young and don't know any better. If they ask me why I look this way I tell them.

June: When I go to the amusement park everyone stares at me. It used to bother me, but now I don't care. I stare back at them.

Myla: I get this all the time: people stare at me and I feel uncomfortable. Basically, I look back at them. If it's little kids I say "Hi," and they walk away. They think I can't talk.

Art: I've had people staring at me because of my disability. It makes me feel unwanted. If it's a child, I tell the parent why I'm in a wheelchair, and then the parent explains to the kid. Sometimes when people look at me strangely, I explain that I was born with a disability called spina bifida which has disallowed me to do some of the other things I want to do, like play football.

Nicole: Once in a mall, a girl stared at me, so I said "Hi." The girl's father said, "Don't talk to her—you might catch it!" Some people in society—maybe one generation in the past—were brought up with that misconception. I was hurt, but I understood. I just said "Bye!"

Al: People have stared at me at the store, on the subway—mostly little kids. I feel a little depressed and definitely angry with them. If a child asks, I may explain, or sometimes not. It depends on how I feel.

These are tough situations to handle. Possibly it helps a little to remind yourself that most staring is *not* malicious. People stare at things and people they aren't used to seeing: women working on telephone lines, male nurses, the school principal in a Halloween costume, an exceptionally beautiful person.

It's small consolation now, but the more people with disabilities get out in public, the less different they will look to others. And the more people are accustomed to seeing people with disabilities, the less they will stare. Increased exposure in the media is helping, too. Films like *My Left Foot;* department store ads showing fashions on people with disabilities; and newspaper comic strips like Lynn Johnston's "For Better or

Worse," in which a teacher is in a wheelchair, are all helping to increase public awareness.

If people ask questions or stare, you don't necessarily owe them an explanation. But every time you explain your disability to a child, one less child will grow up ignorant about people with your disability. And every time you speak to an adult, you help spread the message that people with disabilities have thoughts and feelings, too. Your family can help with your image, too. In Tina's family, for example, her grandmother makes a point of educating others. Tina says, "My grandma has a day care center and when I visit her she has the small kids get close to me, so when they grow up they won't be afraid of people in wheelchairs." Of course, if someone clearly means to tease or ridicule you, it is useless to try to talk to them. Just remember that being a jerk is a far bigger handicap that having a disability.

CHAPTER 5

How Do You See Yourself?

▼ ▼ ▼ ▼ ▼ ▼ ▼ ▼ ▼ ▼ ▼ ▼ ▼ ▼ ▼ ▼

Self-image, or how you feel you look, is an important part of personality. Often, self-image is influenced by how others see you. For example, if you have a girlfriend who thinks you're handsome and clever, you're more likely to see yourself this way. The way others see you frequently depends on the impression you make on them. How you look certainly influences the kind of impression you make, whether it should or not. So we asked:

How do you look, to yourself and others?

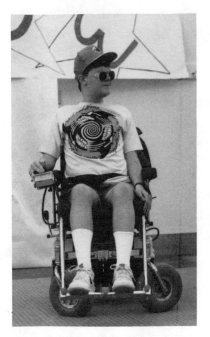

John: I think I make a good impression on others by keeping up my grades, trying to be nice, and trying to be the class clown. Right now I have some pimples, but I have a great smile and I'm kinda handsome.

April: I hope I make a good impression when I first meet a person. I see myself as a short kid with long hair and glasses. I think some of my friends feel sorry for me.

Glen: I've never thought of myself as good-looking. I'm not Mr. America. I'm a normal-looking kid with a few blemishes and hair that never exactly looks right. I impress lots of adults: they say I'm mature. But I think people see me as disabled first. Some people feel uncomfortable—I wish they weren't. I can usually tell if they feel uncomfortable by the way they talk uneasily to me.

Tim: I don't think others accept my disability. I can tell by the way they look at me, like they are just uninterested.

Alyssa: People my own age seem to think I'm funny and nice. Older people usually think I'm older than I am. Overall, I think I make a good impression. I think others see me just like anybody else. My disability doesn't bother others; they just forget about it. How I look to myself depends on how my hair looks and what kind of mood I'm in.

Edward: I feel that people's perceptions differ depending on who it is. Some people are open-minded and accepting.

Sam: Others see me as difficult and not being able to do anything. Some are scared or may be sad about my disability.

June: I try to be myself and not worry about what impression I make or how I look. I worry about the *inside*.

Myla: Basically I look like a child who has a disability she has to live with. My teacher said I am really mature and strong because of my disability. This teacher looks up to me, but I don't know why: I've been this way all my life. But I don't mind people looking up to me!

Art: I don't think others pay attention to my disability. They treat me like a regular human being—like we all should be treated.

Nicole: I think I make a good impression. I want to be known as a person who's nice to others and is happy and raised well by her parents. When I look in the mirror I think I look like my mom, and she's pretty.

Al: I think I look cute, intelligent, and smart.

Tina: I think I look pretty, but I'd like my hair to be lighter. People are positive toward me, partly because of my dog.

Like all teenagers, those with physical disabilities have the usual worries about appearance: hair, skin, weight, clothes. But you have extra obstacles to making a good first impression. Some people may jump to the conclusion that you are mentally retarded because you have impaired speech or spastic movements or simply because you're in a wheelchair. Others may be frightened or uncomfortable, as Glen and Sam mentioned, because you look different or use special equipment, and they don't know how to react.

Part 2 discusses how to help *others* deal with your differences in appearance, speech, or movement. But how do you handle them yourself?

How you choose to look at yourself is really up to you. Do you think first of your leg braces—or of your unusually beautiful hazel eyes? Do you think first of your speech impairment—or of the wise words coming out? It takes a lot of energy and self-discipline to see yourself in a positive light. Naturally, there will be "down" times when you won't be able to do it. Adolescence is the time, after all, when appearances seem to matter most. But you may be more mature on this subject than most teenagers who don't have disabilities, because you may have been through a lot of tough times already.

Most likely, you already realize that, as you get older, looks are not going to be as important to you or others as they seem now. Just think of some of the most influential people of the past and present—Albert Einstein, Eleanor Roosevelt, Mahatma Gandhi, Clara Barton, Mother Teresa, Laurel and Hardy, Bill Cosby. Many of these people weren't or aren't especially good-looking, but were able to achieve great things through their personalities and abilities.

Key   Try to see yourself realistically—to evaluate your strengths and challenges and then use your strong points to offset your weak points. Everybody needs to do this at some time in their life. Part 3 offers some suggestions to help you develop a realistic view of yourself. Although it's easier said than done, it's also important to keep June's advice in mind: try to be more concerned about what's inside and not worry so much about the impression you make or how you look.

This section has dealt with self-perceptions, feelings, frustrations, attitudes. These issues become prominent during adolescence, so some of what we said here may have hit some bull's-eyes with you.

But don't think that once you have reached adulthood you will be a finished product with permanently established ways of seeing yourself and how you fit into the world. Humans are never finished with developing their ideas and outlooks, adjusting relationships, and seeing new paths to building satisfying lives.

While you're growing up, you will want to strive for as much self-knowledge and independence as possible. Although those quests may never again be as strong as they are now, they will not come to an end. They are a big part of what being alive is all about.

ROBERT'S STORY

▼ Robert Watson is thirty, just married, and employed full-time in a meaningful career with a good income. He was in charge of the "Pathways to Independence" mentoring program at United Cerebral Palsy headquarters in Washington, D.C., and currently supervises a dating service for people with and without disabilities. Robert runs his own baseball card business on the side. He grew up on a farm with a large, loving family.

Robert has cerebral palsy and gets around in an electric wheelchair. His hands don't always do what he wants them to do, but he uses a lap-top computer capably. Despite speech difficulties, he makes himself totally intelligible.

Robert cheerfully admits to being a "yuppie" (young, upwardly-mobile professional) and is also pleased to be a "dink" (double income, no kids). His wife has an excellent job, and they live in a house near their jobs in town. But Robert has kept his own trailer home on the family farm "so I won't ever be just a visitor there."

What were some turning points that brought Robert to this successful and satisfying adulthood?

> ▼ A teacher observed him doing well in school. She urged his parents to let him leave a class for children with disabilities and attend his home school. He did, from fourth grade on. His classes there, he says, included "neighbors and cousins and kids who went to church and Bible school with me," and "I was this guy with the walker who walked and talked funny. And that's where I lost my 'Robbie' image and became 'Robert.'"

> ▼ In his early teens, Robert used to ask "Why me?" As he recalls, "Everyone else was playing football; I was on the porch with my Lincoln Logs and Legos. I felt terrible peer isolation. I cried a lot, and I didn't know it then, but I made my mother cry a lot, too."

> ▼ One day, when he was about fifteen, his mother said, "Robert, why don't we focus on what you can do instead of what you can't do?" That was, Robert believes, "my biggest turning point—

I took off like a rocket! And I finally realized that when I came down hard on myself, I came down hard on my family, too."

▼ *Seventh and eighth grades were difficult: he had to "earn respect." He started arm-wrestling, and "kicked their butt through arm-wrestling!" This became a bond with other kids. One day Robert and his best friend were both sent to the principal's office for fighting.*

▼ *His grandparents live in their own home on the farm and Robert often stayed with them on Friday nights. There he played card games for candy and stayed up late with them and their friends. It "got me out of the house and out of my room, being with different people and included in their activities." It took his mother three years to figure out that he phoned his grandmother and asked, "What are you doing tonight?" His grandmother then phoned his mother to say he was invited. Robert still drops in to talk to his grandfather late at night, but "Grandma takes her teeth out at ten o'clock."*

▼ *According to Robert, "If someone hassled me at school, I would one, ignore them; or two, find a common denominator: baseball cards, "Star Trek," or something; or three, run over their toes with my walker to get attention; or four, out-smart them. If someone treats me like a three-year-old, I hit them with my intelligence, then pick them up and talk to them."*

▼ *After he got his driver's license at sixteen, Robert "always had a surplus of girls." He dated one special girl all through high school, then they became "just friends." (Later, in college, girls would sometimes ask him, "Can you make love?" and he would answer, "Sure, I do a good job of it!")*

▼ *Shortly after he graduated from high school, an orthopedist suggested that clipping the heel-cords might improve Robert's gait for walking. The operation would have meant delaying his first year of college. Robert declined. "It was my first independent decision. I told the doctor and my mother, 'I've accepted that I'm going to jump when a dog barks and I'm going to walk like a kangaroo. I've got C.P. and I accept it. Now you accept it.'"*

▼ *College was a 130–mile drive from home, and Robert had fears about taking that long trip alone. At the time, he was mentoring a*

young boy who had picked up fear and a sense of limitations from his mother. Robert got the mother to begin to change her attitude. One day, pushing himself backwards on the floor, Robert got the boy to follow him, bit by bit, and crawl all the way down a long hallway for the first time. Suddenly, Robert realized that "if I thought about my drive home in short sections, it could be reachable and I wouldn't be afraid." Robert still finds this strategy useful. Now, he says, "I have so much to do that if I looked at the whole thing I'd be overwhelmed. I just take it a bit at a time."

▼ Robert's father had counseled him to seek a college degree in the field of computers. But after two years, Robert knew that a career in computers was not for him. He wanted to work with people, not machines. He and his father discussed this disagreement from six o'clock one night until two o'clock the next morning. It was the first time Robert stood up to his father, but he did it "with respect." He told his father, "I want to do this, and I want your blessing." Robert earned his bachelor's degree in social work, and, later a master's degree in social administration.

▼ One day, Robert was in a large indoor farmers' market in the city where he was studying for his master's degree. A few aisles over, he saw an elderly man in an electric wheelchair just like his. He drove over to the man and talked to him, and "he talked just the way I do. Here was this really old guy with C.P. just like me—and I had never thought I'd live past thirty! It was a one-minute change in outlook, and I thought, 'Wow, I'm gonna live!'"

And he is living, to the hilt!

PART 2

▼

GETTING ALONG WITH OTHERS

Getting along with others is a vital part of "making it" in this world. You can't take control over where you are going and where you want to be unless you can communicate with and relate to your family, friends, and people in the community. Obviously, how you relate to others can affect your ability to take charge of your life. For example, if you depend on your parents to get you to and from places, you probably have to arrange your social life around their availability. This dependence makes it harder for you to do things when you want to. Or if you always avoid talking to strangers because you feel shy or have difficulty speaking, you may not pick up the confidence and social skills you will need as an adult. This part of the book is designed to help you understand your relationships better, and to offer some strategies to help you improve them.

CHAPTER 6

YOU AND YOUR FAMILY

▼ ▼ ▼ ▼ ▼ ▼ ▼ ▼ ▼ ▼ ▼ ▼ ▼

Family relationships when you are young can shape your ability to function as an adult. If your family treats you as an equal, contributing member, you are more likely to develop the skills and attitudes you need to succeed. You will learn to value your own abilities and opinions, as well as those of other family members. This will not only give you the self-esteem to try things on your own, but also the security to ask for help when you need it. Healthy relationships as a child can lead to healthy relationships as an adult.

If you come from a family in which it is difficult to cope, it may be harder to learn the skills and attitudes you'll need as an adult. For example, if your parents constantly blame you for things that are out of your control, you may feel misunderstood and angry. Or if you always ask your parents to do everything for you, they may begin to resent the drain on their time and energy. These kinds of emotions can color the way you see yourself and others. You might even end up seeing yourself as less capable than you really are. Of course, most families have occasional problems. But when stress or turmoil is intense or constant, something or someone has to bend.

Your family will not necessarily have more trouble getting along just because you have a physical disability. As you probably already know, many families like yours are exceptionally close and supportive. But having a physical disability can sometimes cause tensions and stresses in relationships. To find out how having a physical disability can affect family life, we asked:

What is your role in your family?

John: My father lives in Germany. I live with my mother and stepfather. My father spoils me. He is too generous—not firm enough. I am a little bit of a troublemaker. I try to be silly around my mom. My stepfather expects me to keep the fun stuff in balance. I'm supposed to feed the pets and get good grades (or my parents will kill me!). I also have to empty the dishwasher.

April: I have a younger brother. I help my mother take care of him. I cook, clean, and do my own laundry. My brother is supposed to clean up after himself, clean up his dishes, and listen to me. He never does!

Glen: My role in the family is being the kid. My responsibilities are to care for my room and not to be destructive. Sometimes I will stick up for my brother in family arguments. My brother will talk to me when he has a problem—much like a friend.

Tim: I am the quiet one in my family. I have an older brother who is also in a wheelchair. My family gets along pretty well. I am supposed to clean my room and make dinner. I am also supposed to be honest. My brother is supposed to look after me. I think he is better than me.

Alyssa: I live with my mother, father, and younger brother. I don't think my family always gets along so well. I avoid talking to my parents; I usually get in trouble or in a fight. My parents think they have the right to overpower me regarding issues such as who I can and cannot see. I used to have chores, but since I work I don't have many anymore. My mother does most of the cooking and cleaning. My brother is irritating, immature, and babyish. Maybe I'll like him better when I'm older.

Edward: I answer the phone for my family. I also clean up the dishes. My sister has no responsibility. She doesn't help at all. That is why I feel so guilty: I can't help and she doesn't. It is not fair.

Timeka: I'm a brat! I like being the only child living at home and I enjoy it to the fullest. I clean up my room, the tub, and the dishes.

June: I feel I am the role model for my two younger sisters. Although I am away at boarding school, I feel that the responsibilities and chores are equally divided among me and my sisters. I get jobs like watching the roast, and my sisters have to carry in the groceries. My sisters complain about that sometimes.

Art: My responsibilities are keeping the peace and vacuuming. Well, now I don't have to vacuum since I work. My sister has to keep her room neat. I think the division of responsibilities is fair, because I don't have to do the chores I used to since I have a job.

Nicole: I have two younger brothers and one younger sister. My brothers and sister argue, but I guess that is a normal family. My role in the family is to raise their spirits when they're sad. I'd love to do chores. My brothers and sister wash dishes, set the table, clean their bedrooms, and make the beds. My brother feeds me. I answer the phone. My sister resents me not doing chores.

Tina: I live with my mother and my dog. Mom and I are like sisters. I'm the little sister and she is the big one who bosses me around. I take out the trash, let the dog out, and keep my room organized.

▼ FAMILY FRICTION

The family lives described above probably sound fairly typical. As in every family, there are occasional disagreements with parents or squabbles with brothers and sisters. But things usually go pretty smoothly. The main difference is that having (or being) a family member with a disability sometimes causes friction. At times, everyone in the family may need to cope with feelings such as resentment, guilt, and embarrassment.

Resentment
▾ ▾ ▾ ▾ ▾ ▾ ▾ ▾ ▾ ▾

Resentment is an emotion that can work in two directions. Your brothers and sisters may resent the "special treatment" you get, at the same time you resent them for being able to do things you can't do. But if you (or they) keep that resentment pent up, feelings are only going to worsen. You may argue or fight constantly, or may not feel like giving one another the kind of emotional support everyone needs. If the resentment and anger are not resolved, the relationship may begin to unravel.

Often there may be resentment from brothers or sisters who don't think you do enough around the house. For example, June explained that while she watched the roast, her sisters had to carry in the groceries. The chores were equally divided, but carrying in the groceries took more actual physical labor. One possible solution to disagreements like this is to ask your brothers and sisters how they think chores could be fairly divided. Perhaps they might be satisfied with small changes in the way responsibilities are shared. For instance, even if you are unable to carry in the groceries, you might be able to help put them away or fold the grocery bags. Or if you can't reach the cupboard to put the dishes away, you may be able to put the silverware in the drawer.

Another suggestion is to have a family council—an informal meeting where all family members can express themselves freely. Each member can tell his side of the story, and then the family can jointly decide what is or isn't fair. Maybe your brothers and sisters really *are* doing too much. Maybe they spend so much time doing housework, running errands, and helping you that they have no time for activities of their own. But if there is no way for you to take up the slack, it may be up to your parents to rethink the way they've assigned responsibilities. Perhaps your family might decide to let some housework slide from time to time to give your siblings a break from chores. It might be better to live with a slightly dirty house than to insist that the dusting, vacuuming, and bathroom cleaning get done quite so often. Or your family could hire a neighborhood kid now and then to mow the lawn or rake the leaves.

Nobody likes to shoulder more than his or her share of a burden. But if you and your family can discuss these matters calmly and rationally, there's a good chance that you can work out a solution that seems more fair.

Sometimes resentment may arise if you seem to get too much of your parents' attention (or money). You may realize that you require a lot of time with your parents because of your daily assistance needs and your many appointments with therapists and doctors. But, how can you explain this to a younger brother who often feels left out? Once again, a

DECISION POINT

Tim's sister, Ann, has cerebral palsy. One summer, Ann required physical therapy five times a week. Because their father worked full-time, Mom had to drive Ann to therapy. This meant Mom usually couldn't drive Tim anywhere, and he had to miss many of his Little League practices and games. Tim resented not being able to go where he needed to go. Sometimes he was angry at his sister for taking up all of Mom's attention. He expressed his anger by spending lots of time in his room alone. When the whole family was home, he retreated to his bedroom. If his family wasn't with him when he wanted them to be, he would not be with them when they wanted him to be.

Weeks went by before Ann asked Tim why he didn't want to do anything with her anymore. After denying several times that there was a problem, Tim finally let all his resentments come pouring out. He told Ann he was sick and tired of family life always revolving around her needs and that he couldn't wait to leave home and go away to college. Ann was stunned. At first she was so upset she could barely speak. Gradually, as her brother continued talking, she began to see that he had a point. "But why didn't you ever *say* anything?" she asked. Tim shrugged. "I didn't want to sound like a whiner," he said.

Ann talked to her mother and the physical therapist and was able to reschedule her therapy appointments for the morning. This freed up Mom's time so she could drive Tim to baseball practice in the after-noon. After that, Ann made a point of periodically asking her brother how he felt, and he was always happy that she asked.

family meeting may help. Discuss your needs related to your disability, as well as other things you want or need. Then have your brothers and sisters explain their wants and needs. For example, perhaps your sister is hurt because your parents can't seem to make it to any of her band concerts, or your brother wishes your father could take him fishing. Or your brothers and sisters may wonder why they can't take swimming lessons, ballet, or a computer class while you "get" to take all kinds of therapy.

See how you and your parents can work together to satisfy as many of the family's wants and needs as possible. Sometimes deciding what the difference is between a want and a need is a good place to start. Do you *need* to have a new wheelchair this year, or do you just *want* one? Does your brother *need* special shoes to be on the track team, or does he just *want* them? Once your family has sorted out the wants from the needs, it may be easier to set priorities. Not everyone will be able to get everything they want, but they may be able to get what is most important to them. Maybe a brother or a sister can go with you to therapy, then afterwards everyone can go on a picnic or watch a soccer game. Or perhaps your parents can set aside a certain time every week to do something with each of your brothers and sisters. Needs related to your disability *are* important, but your brothers and sisters need to be reassured that people care about their needs, too.

Occasionally your brother or sister may be just plain jealous of the special attention you receive from others. What can you do? Talk it out. Explain some of the disadvantages you have to deal with daily because of your disability. For example, it may take you twice as long to get dressed in the morning. But maybe all your brothers and sisters see is the special attention you receive. Share with them some of your struggles.

Thinking about some of the disadvantages of having a disability may fire up your own resentment toward your siblings. Perhaps you sometimes feel down because your brothers' and sisters' lives appear to be much easier than yours. Maybe your sister can drive and you are unable to. Or your brother might be able to get ready to go out in about twenty minutes and it takes you an hour and a half to get showered and dressed. How do you cope with resentment about these kinds of differences?

If you begin to dwell on your disadvantages, try to think of some of your advantages. Chances are there are lots of things that come easier to you than to your brothers or sisters. You may get better grades than your brother, or be the only one who can figure out how to program the VCR, or play a new computer game better than anyone in your family. And when you go to an amusement park, you probably don't have to wait in line for the rides. There are also federal and state laws and regulations that give you certain advantages. For instance, there are special counselors (called Selective Placement Coordinators) whose only job is to help people with disabilities obtain federal employment. And you can often get a discount when you take public transportation. If you list all of the advantages that people with disabilities have, you may find that they help balance the disadvantages.

Feeling left out can also lead to resentment. The teenage years are usually very active years, and your siblings and friends may plan activities that would be difficult for you to participate in. They may take part in skiing trips, camping trips, dances, and foreign exchange student programs. Instead of using your energy in resenting others for being able to do things you can't, why not  figure out some way you could participate? For example, if a ski trip is planned, find out if the lodging is accessible. Call around and ask questions. Could you rent special ski equipment from the National Handicapped Sports Association? When is their annual trip to Hidden Valley? Maybe you could schedule a trip for the same time. Another thing to keep in mind is that all of these activities take a lot of work to coordinate. A good way to get involved and meet people is to volunteer to be on the planning committees.

Guilt
▼ ▼ ▼ ▼ ▼

Guilt is another emotion that can sometimes complicate your family relationships. Like Edward, you may feel guilty because you can't help out around the house as much as you'd like. Or you may sometimes feel guilty about the amount of time your parents spend helping you—lifting your wheelchair in and out of the car or helping you get into bed, for example. If you feel you are being a "burden," guilt can sometimes weigh you down and make you feel inadequate.

Idea   When you are feeling inadequate, it may help to think
             about what you can do, instead of about what you cannot

Decision Point

Jerry, 17, was the second oldest of four children in an active family. Both his mother and father worked. Jerry had always wanted to join the choir at his church but had not mentioned this to his parents. He felt it would just be another hassle for them. After all, practice was at 7 p.m. on Wednesdays and his folks didn't arrive home from work until 6. One day Jerry talked with his friend Melanie about his impossible dream of joining the choir. Melanie didn't see this as an impossibility at all. Why couldn't Jerry make family dinner on Wednesdays and have it on the table when his folks walked in from work? That would allow plenty of time for the meal and the ten-minute drive to the church. It would mean that Jerry would have to organize his homework more efficiently and work out the menu for the night ahead of time. When Jerry proposed the idea to his parents, his mother was skeptical about how Jerry could fix the meal from his wheelchair. But his father was excited about the idea and told Jerry he would help him find ways to maneuver in the old kitchen. In the end, Jerry was able to help his family, and make his dream a reality.

do. So what if you can't vacuum the carpet, mow the lawn, dust the chandelier, or whatever? There are probably many ways you *can* pitch in and make your parents' life easier. For example, your parents may always be exhausted when they get home from work, and the last thing they want to do is cook dinner and clean up. Once in a while you could surprise them and have a pizza delivered for dinner as your treat. Or you could plan out the supper menu for the whole week, write the grocery list, and cut out coupons for your parents to use.

Besides feeling guilty about using your parents' time, you may also sometimes feel guilty about using their money. Wheelchairs, crutches, and leg braces are not cheap. But keep in mind that if one of your brothers or sisters needed braces for their teeth, eyeglasses, allergy medications, or an operation, your family would pull together to come up with the money. Don't feel that you are the only one who needs special equipment; it could be any member of your family at one time or another. Besides, you need your special equipment to get along as independently as possible. Without it, family members would need to devote much more time to helping you.

Sometimes teenagers feel guilty about not being "good enough" in their parents' eyes. They may think their parents deserve to have a child who can do things that they are incapable of. For instance, they may think their parents should have a son who can throw the winning touchdown in a football game, or a daughter who can be the drum major of the marching band. But what you don't realize is that your parents are probably prouder of the accomplishments you have made within yourself than they would ever be if you were a sports star. They know how hard it can be for you to get out of bed knowing that most daily tasks will take you twice as long as others. They know how hard it is for you to keep on trying despite pain, fatigue, and discouragement. Most people will never know what it is like to have a disability and live with it. But you have accepted your disability and moved forward. You are moving beyond your limitations by reaching for realistic goals and taking charge of your life. And that is definitely something to be proud of.

In the end, it is important to realize that it is normal to feel guilty sometimes. It is also important to recognize that there is probably no real reason for you to feel this way. It's not your fault if you can't do as many chores as your brothers or sisters, and it's certainly not your fault if you need special equipment or extra medical care. Both you and your family know that you would likely do anything not to have a disability. Nobody blames you and you shouldn't blame yourself.

Helplessness
▼ ▼ ▼ ▼ ▼ ▼ ▼ ▼ ▼ ▼ ▼

Perhaps you feel, as John does about his father, that your parents should be stricter with you. It could be that they are overprotecting you, or trying to make your life easier by doing things that you could actually do for yourself. For example, they might "take over" whenever you have the slightest difficulty doing a chore, or finish sentences for you if you seem to have trouble expressing yourself. They may also worry excessively about you. Perhaps they ask you to call the second you reach your destination, while your brother doesn't have to call home at all. Or they give you a much earlier curfew than your younger sister has. Being over-protected like this can make you feel helpless. And helplessness can lead to other emotions such as anger, annoyance, and humiliation.

If you feel that your parents baby you too much, there are three steps you can take. First, talk to your parents. Ask them what they expect of you and let them know what you expect of them. Say, for example, "I know you worry about me sometimes, but I wish you would give me the chance to show you I can take care of myself." Your parents may not be aware that they are offending you. That is why clearing the air is so important. Second, if something specific is worrying your parents, you may be able to do something to reduce that worry. For instance, your parents may be worried that your car could break down and you would be stranded. They might worry less if you agreed to call them when you reached your destination. It might also help if you joined an auto club that guarantees its members free towing, or if you got a car phone (assuming you could afford one). Or your parents may worry about you lifting weights because they think you could injure yourself. They might feel better if you promised to get someone to spot for you when you work out. Third, if you want to be treated like an independent person, you need to show others how self-sufficient you can be. Check Part 3 of this book for suggestions on how to do that.

Embarrassment
▾ ▾ ▾ ▾ ▾ ▾ ▾ ▾ ▾ ▾ ▾ ▾ ▾ ▾ ▾

Even if you do everything you possibly can yourself, there still may be some things you can't manage on your own. This means your family may sometimes have to help you when you're out in public. Your mother or father may have to lift you in or out of your wheelchair or feed you. Or one of your parents may have to help you use a public restroom.

If these kinds of situations embarrass you, let your family know. Discuss with them exactly what embarrasses you. Is it the comments strangers make? Is it the tone of voice your parents use when giving you directions? Then try to think of ways to reduce your embarrassment. For example, if it really embarrasses you when a guy your age sees your father pick you up, you could ask him to wait until the boy looks away. Or if it really embarrasses you when your mother reacts negatively to strangers' comments, you could ask her to try a little humor instead. For instance, someone might say, "How can you pick him up? He's so big!"

And your mother could respond with something like: "You know how some farmers in the midwest can pick up a full-grown cow? Well, they pick up that cow every day, starting when it's a calf, so it's really no problem at all!" A response like this might help relieve your embarrassment and also make the person who asked the question think. Humor is a great way to find a "bridge" to others.

Just as your family can sometimes embarrass you in public, you may sometimes embarrass them. Teenaged brothers or sisters are especially easy to embarrass. At this age, kids want to fit in with the crowd—to be just like everybody else. They don't want *anything* out of the ordinary to draw attention to themselves. And that may include unfashionable clothes, a parent who tries to use current slang, or a brother or sister who uses a wheelchair, has spastic movements, or speaks differently.

If your brothers or sisters are embarrassed that you have a physical difference, it can definitely strain your relationship. Maybe your siblings act as if they don't know you when you are out in public. Or maybe they are reluctant to bring friends home to meet you. Obviously, this kind of treatment can really hurt your feelings. It can also make you justifiably angry.

Once again, talk to your brothers and sisters about how you feel and find out how they feel. Be specific. For example, tell your brother, "I felt terrible when you ignored me in the cafeteria today. Why couldn't you at least have said 'hi' to me?" It's possible that your brothers or sisters don't realize how much their behavior bothers you, so airing your grievances may make them more sensitive. It may also help if your brothers or sisters have the chance to talk to other kids who have a family member with disabilities. Just as you can learn coping skills by talking to other kids who are in the same boat as you, so can your brothers and sisters. Sometimes conferences sponsored by disability organizations offer workshops for brothers and sisters. Your brothers and sisters might also be able to find other kids to talk with through organizations such as the Sibling Information Network, listed in the back of the book.

Sometimes it may help to have your brothers or sisters explain to friends ahead of time that you have a disability. This may help relieve the element of surprise. And you can make first encounters more comfortable by making eye contact with people. This makes it less likely that they will end up staring at your crutches or wheelchair. If you are in a wheelchair, you could also ask them to sit down so you can see eye to eye. Remember, not everyone is going to like you—with or without a disability—but that is *their* loss, not yours.

What if you and your family try all the suggestions above, but they just don't work? If family members have been relating to each other one way for years and years, making changes can be difficult. But don't give up. If you and your family can't work out problems on your own, there are many people who can suggest coping strategies and help you deal with your emotions. Try talking to a guidance counselor at school, or perhaps a social worker or a pastoral counselor. If they cannot help you directly, they may be able to recommend a psychologist or other professional who can give you and your family the guidance you need.

There is no step-by-step handbook for solving all the problems your family may encounter. But try to find alternatives to road blocks. Figure out what works best for you. Also remember that you have the freedom and power to interpret events any way you want. Of course, the type of reaction you have may depend on your frame of mind. Some days you will just be better at coping than others. For example, one day you may arrive at school, only to realize that you left your lunch at home and can't remember your locker combination. Next, some jerk runs into you and makes you drop your three-ring binder—which, of course, releases all of your papers in fifty million directions all over the hallway. And then when you get home, your sister complains because she thinks your life is so much easier than hers. In this situation, you will most likely say something we don't want to print here. However, on another, more peaceful day, you may feel like discussing other ways you and your sister could divide the household chores.

CHAPTER 7

YOUR FRIENDS

▼   ▼   ▼   ▼   ▼   ▼   ▼   ▼   ▼

Pick a TV sitcom . . . any sitcom. Isn't it incredible the way the kids on these shows talk to their parents about *anything* and *everything?* They have heart-to-heart talks with their parents about peer pressure at school, premarital sex, alcohol, drugs, AIDS—you name it. But in real life, most teenagers are not quite that open with their parents. There are probably some things that you just don't feel comfortable discussing with your parents. In fact, the older you get, the less you will probably rely on your parents for support. As you start to expand your world beyond your family, you will likely come to depend more and more on a support network of friends. This is a natural part of growing up. To become as independent as possible, you have to start finding sources of emotional and physical support outside the family.

Having a disability doesn't necessarily make it harder to make or keep friends. According to the folks interviewed for this book, a lot depends on your personality and on finding someone with qualities you value. A friend will find interest in what you have to share. To get an idea of how having a disability may affect friendships, we asked:

What are your friendships like?

John: At my new school, there's only one other wheelchair. I'm becoming friends with a senior, with a girl, and with some of my teachers. I don't make friends very easily. Being shy keeps me away from people I want to meet—it's a mental problem I've had for years. Most of my friends are people who were in special classes with me, but some are from my neighborhood. My friends and I mostly talk. We try to get together at the mall, movies, carnivals, sleep-overs, summer programs, and parties. What I look for in a friend is someone who can understand me and doesn't look at the surface but at what's inside. I look for someone who has the same interests and the same qualities.

April: I make friends at school, at camp, at work, and at the mall, of course—that's where we hang out. I may go up to someone and introduce myself and just go on from there. Sometimes they have come up to me. Some of my friends have disabilities, some don't. I look for someone who's fun to hang around with, easy to talk to, and likes the same things I like. I think some of my friends feel sorry for me.

Glen: Most of my friends are from school and some are from church. Most are not disabled because I've been mainstreamed. I may make friends with a stranger I'm sitting next to in class, or sometimes by being introduced by other friends. I look for someone who's nice, has some humor (some don't)—and also is aware of me and the things I can and cannot do. We go to the movies and talk on the phone a lot. Talk basically is the thing I do most with friends.

Tiffany: My friends all have disabilities and are almost all from school. I can be friends with people who are nice and caring, and who talk or sign to me.

Tim: To make friends you have to break the ice, say "Hi," talk about feelings, express your own feelings. Some kids may say, "Oh, there goes a guy in a wheelchair." But just go ahead. Talk to yourself. Say, "I can do it." Try to have a girlfriend—don't worry about the consequences. It takes a lot of guts. Look into your heart and brain. Try to give it your best. Set goals for yourself and give yourself time to achieve goals. Some will admire your struggle, and they can be your friends.

Alyssa: I don't especially try to make friends, but sometimes I reach out, and sometimes others make the first approach. Friends are from school, parties, and places I hang out on the weekends. We may go to people's houses, go shopping, or have parties. A friend is someone I can have fun with and someone I can trust.

Edward: I don't usually go looking for friends because I'm shy. Usually I make friends when I help them with something, in school or other places I go. I can be friends with someone I can talk to and who will listen to me—someone I can do things with. We may just talk or go to the movies.

Timeka: I've never had to "make" friends; they come to me like a magnet. They call me after school. I'm the only person at my school in a wheelchair. I look for honesty and trust in a friend. I look for someone I can talk to when things aren't going so well. We enjoy talking on the phone, spending the night, and going shopping and to the movies.

Sam: Girls like me because I'm cute; boys like me because they like the wheelchair. I make friends at school, in the neighborhood, and at the community center. I may go over to their houses or be in after-school activities with them. A friend to me is someone with a nice attitude who is helpful and gives me reassurance.

June: To make friends I may go up and introduce myself. If you are mad at the world it will show; I try to stay happy so people will get to know me. My friends, with and without disabilities, are from school. We like to go out or to the movies or parties. My definition of a friend is someone who knows everything about you and still likes you. I hope others will see me as a good friend who may be a little bit different.

Sometimes others worry they may be doing something I can't handle. I can usually tell if they are worried because they will look at me funny. Like they will put out one arm to help me up a curb, when I don't need it. Sometimes people will treat me differently or special. Like if I am on a walk with someone, I can tell they are walking slower just for me. Usually after a long walk, everyone will assume I must be so tired, when actually I'm fine. When people try to help me and I do not need it I will speak up and say, "No, that's OK—I got it." I do not feel I take advantage of my disability, but my friends sure take advantage of it. If they go out and there is a long line, my friends will tell me to go on up in the line. I don't. I don't like to draw attention to myself.

Myla: My friends are mostly from school and camp. They are both with and without disabilities, maybe more without. I make friends by talking to people, getting to know them, and letting them know me. We usually go to the mall, go swimming, and to the movies. To me, a friend is someone who is nice and funny—someone I can get along with and share my thoughts and feelings with.

Art: I make friends by telling them a little bit about me and who I am. This could be at school, at work, at home, at activities, or at sports events. We like to go to the mall, to movies, stay out late. I look for friends who are trying to be all they can be.

Nicole: I have lots of disabled friends from being in a special school program for so many years, plus non-disabled friends from when I've been mainstreamed, as I am now. I also have friends from church and Girl Scouts. We like to do the usual things: go to the mall, birthday parties, out to dinner, and to movies, and I have lots of phone conversations, especially with friends who aren't in my new school with me. I think a friend is someone who's not interested in appearance, like a snazzy wheelchair—someone who will accept you and not be ashamed of you or feel sorry for you. I don't want to be treated differently!

Others have just accepted me as one of the crowd, which I never expected! I can tell they accept me because they speak to me in a natural way and they don't tailor their activities to suit me. I think there are some times I could take advantage of having a disability, but I don't always enjoy doing that. I just do it when it's best for me.

Al: I have a lot of friends, but it's not very easy to make friends. I usually just start a conversation. I make friends at work and in synagogue youth groups, and a lot are from school. We talk on the phone, go out to eat, and play wheelchair tennis. What I look for in a friend is intelligence—plus other things, depending on the person's sex.

Tina: My dog, a Canine Companion, attracts people. I may greet them and say "Hi." My friends are from school, the neighborhood, and church. In the neighborhood we walk around or go up to the grocery store, play games, hang out. We talk on the phone. When church friends visit we do stuff inside: listen to the radio, play Nintendo. I think a friend is someone who is helpful, kind, willing, and likes *me*, not just my dog.

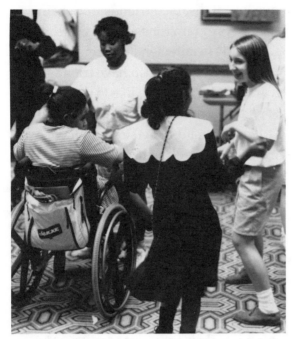

Your friendships, like those described above, are probably pretty normal in most respects. But you may also find that some friends treat you differently. As June notes, some friends might worry that you can't keep up, or might offer help that you don't need. Or as April observes, some of your friends might feel sorry for you. To get your friends to stop the special treatment, it helps to understand why they may treat you as they do.

Misjudging Your Abilities. If your friends don't understand what you are able to do, they will not know what to expect of you. As a result, they may give you a lot of unnecessary help, overprotect you, or avoid doing certain activities with you. For example, your friends may get upset when someone lightly bumps into you in the hall. Or they may get angry when others stare at you in public. Or one friend may always want to get your books or your lunch for you, when actually you can do this yourself.

Most likely, your friends treat you this way because they care about you and don't want you to get hurt. They may think they are saving you the embarrassment of admitting you can't do something. But in reality they may have jumped to the wrong conclusion.

You can easily clear up these misunderstandings by communicating your abilities. Tell your friends what you can and can't do. Be specific. For example, tell them: "I can dress myself," "I do my own hair and nails," "I am able to push myself in my chair," "I know what to say to jerks who stare," and "I'm a very strong swimmer." What may seem obvious to you may not be to them. Stating your abilities up front will help your friends understand that in most cases you are not fragile. If you have osteogenesis imperfecta, and your bones *are* fragile, it is even more important to let people know your physical limitations.

Maybe you are worried about hurting your friends' feelings. If so, try letting them know that allowing you to do things for yourself is sometimes a better way to show their caring. For example, tell them: "How about letting me do the complaining next time? I'm trying to work on my assertiveness." Perhaps you might want to have one simple rule with your friends to put everyone at ease: If you need help, you will ask for it. They don't have to try to read your mind. And although you appreciate their caring, don't let them think they need to be responsible for you.

Pitying You. Sometimes friends may pity you. As a result, they may be excessively nice to you or they may be afraid to upset you or get mad at you. Perhaps they do special favors for you, such as always letting you choose what movie to watch or what kind of pizza to order. Or maybe they put up with your bad moods without complaining, even if you hurt their feelings.

Your friends might feel sorry for you for several reasons. First, they may be thinking about how they would feel if they had a disability like yours. They have no idea how they would cope in your situation, so they may assume you feel the same way. Second, they may be focusing on what you *can't* do, rather than on what you *can* do. They might think about the sports and outdoor activities you might not be able to do, and not even stop to think about all the other things you excel in. Third, they may know little or nothing about your disability, or may be misinformed about it. As a result, they might think things are going to get a lot worse than they are, that you are in constant pain, or that your disability is harder to cope with than it is. Finally, some friends might feel sorry for you if you seem to feel sorry for yourself.

Once again, the solution is to be direct with your friends. Tell them that you want to be treated like all their other friends: You are strong and you can take it. If they are uninformed about your disability, offer to answer their questions, or give them information to read. Let your friends know that when people pity you, it makes you feel like a small child, unable to do things for yourself.

If you constantly do everything you are capable of doing by yourself, you will not fall into a parent-to-child relationship with your friends. Be confident of your capabilities. Don't be afraid to stand up for yourself. You have value.

▼ .... ▼

Decision Point

Eileen and Janelle and Donna talked back and forth on the phone about the ninth grade dance. Would any boys invite them? Maybe Donna would be invited because she only needed a walker, while Eileen and Janelle had to use wheelchairs. If nobody asked them out, should they still go? Should they go as a group, the three of them? And what should they wear? The conversations went on for weeks.

On the big night, the three friends were at the dance together. They stayed on one side of the gym where most of the other ninth grade girls were. Most of the boys were on the opposite side. In the middle, about seven couples were dancing. Mostly boys talked to boys and girls talked to girls. Eileen and Janelle and Donna stuck together, but a few other girls came over and talked with them, too. The refreshments weren't bad, and the gym looked festive with balloons and streamers. The band was surprisingly good.

When they talked on the phone the next day, the friends decided that that they had probably had as good a time as any other girls at the dance. And Andy Peterson, a tenth grader they all admired, had said "Hi" to them as they left the gym. All in all, it had been worth it.

▼ .... ▼

Seeing Your Disability First. One final reason that friends—especially new friends—may treat you differently is that they have trouble seeing past your disability. They may see you first as a disabled person rather than as someone who happens to have a disability. Even when you are sitting down, they may not be able to forget that you use crutches or a wheelchair. As a result, they may treat you differently than they do others. For example, they may be extra careful about what they say around you, for fear they may offend you. Often, the best solution is to let them know how you would like to be treated, then be patient until they get to know you. The teenagers we interviewed suggested several other ways to deal with this problem when we asked:

What do you do when people focus too much on your disability?

John: I prove to them that I'm not as disabled as they thought. I try to talk to them.

April: I don't know. I just talk to them. I tell them, "Don't look at the crutches, look at the person. It's inside that counts, not outside." At first when I meet someone new they ask me questions like do I need this or that. Then after awhile they don't see any crutches.

Glen: I let people know me. They see the wheelchair first, so I can't help someone *not* see the disability.

Edward: I don't do anything. If they want to see me as a disabled person, that's their problem.

Timeka: I don't discuss what I have. I just hang out, blend in.

Sam: I don't know. If I explain the whole thing, they see it.

Myla: I try to act like everyone else. I'm going to try; if I can't do it, I'll get help.

Art: I tell them to just think of me as a regular human being without a wheelchair, crutches, or a scooter!

Al: I just talk to them.

Decision Point

Tori was one of six juniors at her school who was voted to run for Junior Prom Queen. Honored at being chosen, Tori decided to run, even though she hadn't been asked to the Prom. She figured that if she won, *someone* would invite her. True, she couldn't dance that well with her braces and crutches, but she knew she could have a great time with the right guy.

(Continued)

The day after the election, Cecilia, who was on the ballot counting committee, met Tori at her locker. "You didn't buy a formal, did you?" Cecilia asked. Tori knew that Cecilia was telling her she hadn't won. Tori was devastated. She couldn't help thinking that the reason she had lost was because she had a disability. To top it all off, nobody asked her to the Prom.

It didn't help when Tori's parents tried to comfort her by pointing out that four other girls had also lost the election for Prom Queen. At least *they* had dates. Clearly, everybody was seeing her disability, not her. She felt frustrated that this was a situation she couldn't take charge of. There was only so much she could do to influence everyone's opinions of herself.

CHAPTER 8

HOW ABOUT BUILDING A BRIDGE?

▼ ▼ ▼ ▼ ▼ ▼ ▼ ▼ ▼ ▼ ▼ ▼

How you feel about interacting with people you don't know probably depends more on you than on your disability. Some people are just naturally more outgoing. They don't hesitate to ask strangers for directions, request help, or explain their needs. Shy people, on the other hand, often go out of their way to avoid speaking to strangers, unless it's an emergency. One kind of personality is not "better" than the other. But if you have a physical disability, you might sometimes have to *act* outgoing even if you're really shy at heart.

There are times you have to interact with people you don't know to get what you need. Many items in stores and other public places may be out of your reach: pay phones, bookshelves, groceries, vending machines. And some buildings, or parts of buildings, may be completely inaccessible to you unless someone carries you or moves furniture out of your way. All of these obstacles can be quite annoying. The trick is to learn to deal with strangers in a way that helps minimize the annoyances and enhances your independence.

For some insight on how other teenagers handle themselves in the community we asked:

How do you deal with strangers?

April: I have to deal with strangers a lot. Like if I can't reach something in a store, I ask for help. Or if I'm riding in my wheelchair and I fall out, I have to ask for help. I usually try to look for a friendly person. If I can't find anyone just walking around, I usually look for someone who works in the store. I feel OK about asking someone I don't know for help.

Nicole: I introduce myself to strangers. If I need help at school, I usually ask girls.

Al: A cab driver once told me I am handicapable. Others are not so accepting and may feel I am not independent.

Tina: They think I am fragile and they might break me. Others think what I have is contagious. In school I get help with some things. One advantage is that I get to go to the front of the lunch line.

How do you feel about asking for help in public places? Embarrassed that you can't do something yourself? Angry that things are out of your reach? Afraid that you might be imposing on someone? Resentful that people don't automatically help you when they see you struggling? Perhaps you feel one way in one situation and another way in another situation.

The fact is, you should never feel hesitant about telling strangers what you need. After all, it is not your fault that the elevator is broken, or that a store was set up so that it is inaccessible, or that the counters are too high for you to see over. You have as much right to shop, eat, attend school, work, worship, ride the bus, attend movies and plays, participate in recreation programs, and just plain *live* in the community as anyone else. By law, businesses and other establishments are required to serve you. And that includes giving you whatever special assistance you might need. The interview with David Capozzi in the Appendix explains more about the law that guarantees you these rights—the Americans with Disabilities Act of 1990 (ADA).

Of course, just because you have a right to be in the community doesn't mean it will always be easy to ask for help. But the alternative may be to go away frustrated. For example, if you can't reach a book on the top shelf in the library, you have two choices. Either you can ask someone to reach it for you, or you can settle for a less-desirable book on a lower shelf. If someone is in the aisle, you could ask them for help. Let people know exactly what you need; be specific. Say, "I want the hardcover copy of *The Catcher in the Rye*." Or, in a grocery store, "I want to read the ingredients in both brands of cake mix before I decide which one I want."

Actually, people are often happy when you request their assistance. They may have felt uncomfortable watching you struggle, but didn't know how you would react to their help. Also remember that you can always request help from employees. They are paid to assist their customers, with and without disabilities.

Possibly the worst situation to encounter is a non-accessible bathroom. What are your options? Evaluate the situation. Do you have time to look for another bathroom? Is there someone you know nearby who could help you? If not, are you willing to ask a stranger for help? These are questions you need to answer yourself in order to best meet your needs. After you have decided what to do, always inform the management about their problem. Ask them how they will resolve this situation so it won't happen to anyone else. Explain your concerns in a calm manner. Follow up your concerns by a letter to the store or restaurant. For more on building accessibility, see the interview with Mark Mazz in the Appendix.

Obviously, it can be hard to keep your temper if you are prevented from doing something so important as using a public restroom. But you usually will get the best results if you are polite. Many times an employee is not to blame for a particular situation. It is not the waiter's fault if your steak is too rare, and it is not the salesclerk's fault if the doorway to the dressing room is too narrow. If you explain the problem politely, people will be more likely to want to figure out a solution for you.

Politeness is also important when you're in a crowd. For instance, have you ever eaten at a restaurant where all the tables were so close together you had to weave around to search for a path? If people are in your way, consider tapping their shoulders and asking if they could slide their chair further under the table. People prefer to be asked to move rather than being bumped into. When people are walking in a crowd around you, having someone walk in front of you is sometimes helpful in clearing a path. If you are going to a concert or sports event, ask about reserved seating for persons with disabilities. This seating is usually located close to an exit and restrooms. Usually it is in a spot where you can see the event while sitting down.

For advice on communicating with strangers, see the next chapter. For information on refusing unwanted help from strangers and being assertive, see Part 3.

CHAPTER 9

IS TALKING HARD FOR YOU?

▼ ▼ ▼ ▼ ▼ ▼ ▼ ▼ ▼ ▼ ▼ ▼ ▼ ▼

As this section of the book stresses, one of the keys to successful relationships is clear and open communication. But what if your disability makes it difficult or impossible to speak so others can understand you? If you have problems with the physical process of communicating, it can affect your ability to relate to others. Like the teenagers below, you might have more trouble communicating in some situations than others.

How do you handle speech difficulties?

John: I'm flip-flopping about saying things right out to others. It depends on whether it's an old or a new friend. Most people understand my speech, but sometimes they say "speak up" and I have to repeat. Keeping my pitch lower helps. I sometimes use a little sign language, but 99.9 percent of the time I talk. It is easier for me to talk to people in person; I don't use the phone much.

Tiffany: I use sign language, but it is difficult because I can't use my left hand. I also use a little speech at times, gestures, and written messages. I'm trying out different language machines to choose the best one for me.

Sam: I speak up, but I'm nervous talking to girls at school. I'll get her phone number and call her. With boys, some I can handle in person, some on the phone. I work on my speech problems with the speech therapist at school.

▼ Communicating with Family and Friends

If you have trouble speaking, it can lead to other problems. For example, you might come to rely on your parents to act as your interpreters. This could make it harder for you to be independent when you're out in the community. It could also limit the kinds of relationships you are able to have. After all, how would someone realize you're worth getting to know if you can't tell them what you think? In addition, there may be times when you don't feel comfortable discussing something with your parents. But if they are the only ones who understand your speech, who else can you turn to?

It is OK to rely on your family to assist you in communicating. But also try to find a few friends who are willing to learn to understand you. Let them know that you don't mind if they ask you to speak slower or to repeat something over and over. This may be frustrating for you and for them. Be patient and persistent, and keep it simple. And don't accept less of an interpretation than what you really mean. For example, if you want chocolate, don't settle for vanilla.

There is another potential problem related to speech difficulties: Sometimes, even though you are really mad or depressed, you might feel that it takes too much effort to try to express yourself. This is a problem for several reasons. First, your emotions don't go away just because you don't express them. In fact, they may eat at you more and more if you can't or won't share them with someone. Second, many people would probably be happy to help figure out solutions to what is troubling you. But they can't read your mind and won't know that something is bothering you unless you let them know. What can you do?

If speaking is very difficult, you could try letting others know how you feel through facial expressions or body language. If you have some control of your voice, use vocal intonation to help get your meaning across. You can use changes of pitch, not just words, to help listeners understand that you are expressing displeasure, asking a question, or making a joke. Or you can try raising the volume of your voice at important points in your conversation. Another solution is to write notes to others explaining what you mean. A talking machine or computer could also assist you in speaking. As John Staehlin and James Mueller discuss in the Appendix, scientists are constantly working on technological improvements to communication devices. For more information, contact the International Society for Augmentative and Alternative Communication listed in the Resource Guide. Sometimes insurance companies may pay for some communication equipment.

▼ Communicating in the Community

In the community, you may have many of the same communication problems that you have with friends and family. But you might also have other, even more frustrating problems. If you use sign language, for example, strangers may assume you are deaf. They may speak to your companions, not you, or shout when they talk to you. Even if you don't use sign language, people may assume you can't understand them simply because you are in a wheelchair.

If someone is with you, instruct them to tell others straight out that you are not deaf. At school or at work, you can sometimes set up a simple sign that reads "I'm not deaf. Please don't yell at me." This sign can make it easier to deal with people who assume that anyone who has difficulty speaking can't hear or understand normal speech. You can also carry pre-printed cards that explain that you have difficulty communicating. The cards could state your name and explain that you have difficulty in speaking, are able to hear, and would like to communicate.

Another problem you may face is that many people have no experience communicating with somebody who has trouble speaking. People who can talk are sometimes shy of those who can't. They may avoid talking to you, or look in the other direction when you speak. Remember that your eyes, your facial expression—your whole manner— let people know how you feel about yourself and your disability. They also convey your tolerance of people who don't know how to deal with you. You can look directly at others with an accepting, open expression that says, "Hey, I'm a person too!" Maybe it shouldn't be up to you to approach others, but often it is either that or no contact at all. Instead of taking offense, you may have to take the offensive. You may have to be the one who says hello—pleasantly, not aggressively—and tries to find some common interest to talk about. Sometimes you won't have the energy to take that first step, and that's OK, too. If you do, it won't work every time, of course, and you may feel shunned. But it will work some of the time.

Some strangers may get frustrated and impatient trying to understand you. Let them know that you are experiencing frustration too—perhaps by using gestures, facial expressions, or vocal intonation, as described above. Let them know that what you have to say is most definitely worth waiting for! Humor is often a good way to break the ice with a stranger.

Perhaps you may want to use a different form of communication in the community than you do at home. For example, you might usually use speech with friends and family who are used to your speech patterns. But in a store, it might be quicker to use a message board to tell a clerk what you need. Once again, you know what is best for you. Experiment with different ways of communicating until you find the most effective one. And don't give up speech therapy. Small improvments may make a big difference in being understood. Even mature actors continue to work on their speech or adjust it for a particular role. Remember that a speech and language pathologist can help you select and use augmentative devices like communication boards or computerized speech in addition to helping you improve your speech, language, and voice.

SUZANNE'S STORY

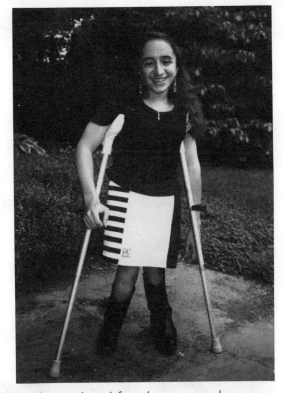

▼ Suzanne Richard is a senior theater/acting major at the University of North Carolina, Chapel Hill. She has osteogenesis imperfecta and uses crutches and sometimes an electric wheelchair to get around. She lives with one roommate in an apartment off campus.

Susie has had about 120 broken bones in her lifetime, mostly when she was younger. (Her last was encountered in a sledding spree during her sophomore year in college.) She is four feet tall.

Susie is the youngest of four children. The Richard family is very close and well-traveled; Susie spent her early years in France, where her father was stationed with an American company. They also spent time in Canada before returning to the United States when Susie entered first grade.

In her Canadian kindergarten, Susie says, "I was a terror, a nightmare." She remembers the teacher taking her crutches when she hit a boy who had stolen her cowboy gun and her cowboy hat. In her own defense she says, "He hit me first!" She was a tomboy and related better to boys than to girls.

She remembers another incident in grade school when she had been picking on an "obnoxious" boy. He turned to her, saying, "Shut up, you stupid, short, handicapped person!" The teacher and other students were shocked at the boy. "I remember being shocked, too. It was the first time I had been picked on for being disabled."

In the fifth grade, Susie stopped having boyfriends. She says, "My boyfriend, Luke, walked in saying 'I love Heather Rogers.'" Susie began matchmaking then, setting up Heather with Luke.

Susie remembers her transition from grade school to junior high as a traumatic time. In the sixth grade she was Miss Popularity. She assumed she would be going on to junior high with her class. But her "home" junior high was not accessible, so she was sent to another school that was. In that in-between summer, she also had back surgery. She found the new school to be cliquey and she felt awkward and like an outsider. She did know one person, however, and they slowly developed a small group of friends.

In high school the class was split and sent to two different schools. Susie chose the school with the better drama department. There were no cliques; everyone seemed to fit in. The drama department was great and "took me in" reports Susie. Between her sophomore and junior years, she spent ten days touring Europe with classmates on the track team.

During this time, Susie says she thought little about her disability. "No one seemed to care."

Soon, Susie began dealing with what guys thought of her. Whenever one acted interested in her, she would wonder what he saw in her, or wonder if he was a "loser" because he was interested in her. She says, "I wondered what others thought of the guy before I judged him for myself." She also says she used to "throw myself at guys, then get scared, back off, and do the opposite. I would put a boy on a pedestal, then he'd turn out

not to be perfect. I would get timid, feel stupid, and the wall would go up."

She dated and had a "disastrous relationship," after which she began to feel insecure and wasn't sure who to trust. This was a new feeling for Susie because boys had always been her best friends. She continued to date, however. She attended school dances and special school celebrations like Homecoming.

As she has grown older, Susie's feelings about guys have changed. Now she feels there is no reason she shouldn't be attracted to another person and no reason why he shouldn't find her attractive.

Susie's family has helped shape her view of herself and her disability. "My mother always said I was the sweet one . . . and then I hit the teens! My brothers and sister, being older, taught me everything. They wouldn't teach me about being disabled; they taught me about regular growing-up things. Growing up was easier on me than on my brothers and sister. They had to struggle to have anything special about them. I always felt very special. I could always do anything I wanted. I never felt in competition with my sibs. I love my relationships with my sibs even more now. They give honest answers and I value their opinions more now."

"The issue of disability never came up when I was younger, although my family would go to OI (osteogenesis imperfecta) meetings." Then, in her early teens, her brother joked about her disability. She remembers him saying, "Your arms are so long they're like gorilla arms." This was something she had always known, but had never heard anybody say. At the time, she recalls, she couldn't take it. But now she says, "It was my problem. I had to learn to deal with it. People are oversensitive about being disabled."

Today Susie jokes with her brothers and sister about having a disability. But, she admits, getting "an accurate self-image" was not easy. She says, "I always lived in my imagination. Self-concept is hard to think about. It's taken awhile to get honest with myself about how I look. I'm a perfectionist, like to be the best, outstanding. I accentuate the parts that are better. Most people don't look like Julia Roberts!"

Besides her family support, Susie credits two activities with helping her discover her strengths and talents: involvement in the theater and her summer employment.

"Theater helped me," she says. "I always loved myself a bunch but was also self-critical. I see myself as attractive now."

Susie has played leading roles throughout her high school and college careers, at a special summer drama workshop, and at the John F. Kennedy Center for the Performing Arts in Washington, D.C.

During her college career, Susie appeared in "Beauty Secrets," a play about how beauty affects image and how women think about themselves. Susie played the role as a woman with a disability. "No one in the department thought of me as a disabled person." Susie found it interesting to watch the way people treated her after the play. "A lot of people treated my character as more disabled than I am! My friends wanted to know what was me and what was script. I was making more of a statement about myself, more personally out on a limb."

She has found surprisingly few barriers in the theater. Once, however, a professor in a high school summer drama course (himself disabled) suggested she "get into another line of work" because she had a disability. Susie became angry, stayed in the course, and won applause for her final audition. A professional actress with a disability advised Susie that she would "have to be better, not just as good as everyone else."

Her summer work as a secretary for a national volunteer organization has also helped Susie uncover her assets. "I am an interesting person," she says. "The job helped me see that. I feel more assertive, in control. I'm still ditzy and procrastinate, but people can trust me, depend on me."

When Susie isn't on stage, at work, or in class, she likes to needlepoint, read science fiction and fantasy, write poetry and plays, go to movies or watch TV, and party!

Her plans for the future are to live in Los Angeles or New York, get an apartment with a friend, go to graduate school in theater, and . . . star as an actress.

PART 3

▼

HOW CAN I GET WHERE I WANT TO GO?

To be a teenager, dreaming of the future, means "trying on" different jobs . . . educations . . . friendships . . . geographical settings . . . styles of dressing . . . so you can decide how you can make your life the way you want it to be. The challenge to you is to begin to pick up the reins, to begin directing your life. To take charge.

The first part of this job (let's face it, this is hard work!) is to take control of your life by beginning to analyze yourself—to inventory what's in stock and what's missing.

To get you started, this part of the book will help you explore:

- What independence means to *you*.
- How to figure out how independent *you* are.
- How to decide what strengths and challenges *you* have.
- How your disability affects *your* life.
- How and when *you* ask for help.
- How to let others know when *you* don't need help.
- What expectations *you* have of yourself.
- What expectations *others* have for you.
- How to resolve the conflict when *you* have different expectations for yourself than others have for you.
- How and when to speak up for *yourself*.

Having this information about yourself and some tips on how to use this knowledge will enable you to begin making decisions about your life. Good decisions will help you to lay the groundwork for the future you want to build for yourself. They will help you to *take charge!*

CHAPTER 10

TAKING STOCK: HOW INDEPENDENT ARE YOU?

▼ ▼ ▼ ▼ ▼ ▼ ▼ ▼ ▼ ▼ ▼ ▼ ▼ ▼ ▼

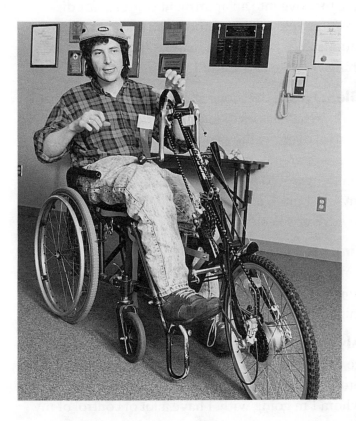

Being independent is not an all-or-nothing proposition. Most people are independent in at least some areas of their lives, no matter how dependent they may be in other areas. Often, too, how independent you feel depends on how you look at it. If you want to reach for more independence, though, it helps to figure out where you are starting from. That is, before you can think about how independent you might be in the future, it's important to assess the amount of independence you feel you have now. To get a feel for some of the many forms independence can take, we asked:

What is independence?

How independent are you?

John: My parents make all decisions for me, but they're trying to discuss choices with me. I think I'm about 60 percent independent now, and that I could be almost totally independent eventually. Being able to do the things normal people take for granted, and being the best I can be would mean independence to me.

April: I make some decisions for myself, but my mom and grandparents have to make some decisions for me. Independence to me would mean being able to go out by myself with friends, without my mother; having the house to myself; cleaning up without being told; going to work by myself. I'd like to move into an apartment complex for disabled people and cook and clean and do my own laundry. . . . But I'm not mature enough to do the things I'd like to do, and I'm scared.

Glen: I make decisions about what to wear, what to do, what classes to take, but I don't have as much control over my life as some kids. I like someone else—a parent— having a little control. Being independent would mean being able to take care of myself. I think I'll be more independent when I get my driver's license.

Tim: I feel I have a lot of control over my life, but I'm not very independent. Fear of falling and getting hurt keeps me from being as independent as I might be.

Alyssa: I've made many decisions: about where to go to high school, choosing to be in a work-study program, where I'm going when I go out and whom I'm going with. I have a lot of control of my life, but my parents also have control. I still live with my parents, but I pay for my clothes and live pretty independently. If I had more money I could be more independent.

Edward: I have more control of my life mentally than physically. My parents have control. I have to do exactly what my father says. They think they are helping me, but sometimes they get in my way. My independence is limited because I need people to get me places; I can't drive yet. I do make decisions about what I want to do, such as what classes I want to take in college, but I let others sign up for me.

Timeka: I'm very independent except for driving. I make decisions about going places, attending meetings, buying something, what I want to do with my life. Sometimes I feel more grown-up than other teens my age because I do more than they do, actually.

Sam: I feel about 50 percent independent; I'm still working on it. My parents and teachers control the other half.

June: If you don't look out for yourself, no one else will. I have control. At boarding school I feel that I run my life. I make decisions about college, friends, school, and guys. Boarding school has helped me grow up faster and become a stronger person inside. Of course, my parents have control over my life, too. True independence will be when I can be on my own comfortably, with minimal aid . . . and when I'm older, out of school, and have my own family life.

Myla: My parents (definitely my parents!) and God, too, have control over my life. I probably have about 50 percent control over it myself: choosing what I have money for when shopping, what I want to wear, and which friends I want to talk to, for example. Having a disability has made me grow up a lot faster than other kids, but sometimes I'm silly and act kind of stupid. I feel I could be pretty independent if I really tried. I feel pretty independent right now. But my disability holds me back sometimes. I can't go places with my friends by myself because my mom's afraid I'll get hurt.

Art: Independence means freedom to me, and I already feel pretty independent. My mother and father—and my sister—have some control over my life, but I make decisions about what I want to do, like going out. And I actually feel more grown up than other people my age.

Nicole: I have some control over my life and make decisions about things like time management and attending my home school. But teachers, parents, friends, and most of all God have control over my life. I feel satisfied that I'm grown up in my own way for my age. I'm not a nerd but I'm not the most popular girl in school either. Some friends are so hip-hop about begin cool and want to be accepted so badly that they don't care what it takes. I'm satisfied to know my life isn't public property. Physically I have to depend on a lot of people for most things. Mentally I'm pretty independent. And socially I'm a social patriot: I will stand up for what I believe in.

Al: My control over my life is about 70 to 80 percent. My parents, my brother, my boss and co-workers control the rest. Most of the time I feel as grown up as others my age because I can make decisions, think like most other people, and do things by myself. I could be more independent, and maybe I should be, but I live with my mom and dad and just haven't let go.

Tina: I'm in charge of my grades, my dog, my wheelchair, my personal needs, my room, and my free time. I choose my friends, where I want to go, what I want to wear. My mother, teachers, and assistant also have control. I hang out with older kids; they accept me for what I am. So I feel more mature than other people my age. Being truly independent would mean being able to fend for myself, do stuff by myself, and make decisions.

Obviously, independence can be described in many ways. Some of these ways include:

- Freedom
- Making your own decisions
- Having control, power
- Choosing your own friends
- Deciding what to wear
- Doing what you want to do
- Doing things without your parents
- Taking care of yourself
- Paying your own way

Independence is also something that can be present to different degrees in different areas: mental, physical, or emotional. For example, like Edward, you might feel that you are completely in control of your thoughts, but not of your body.

Limitations to your independence can come from two main sources:

- other people, and
- your own physical limitations

Parents and teachers are mentioned most often as limiting independence. But there may be others who have a lot of control over *your* life.

Common physical limitations that can reduce independence include fear of injury and inability to drive. Perhaps there are other specific needs in your life that you feel hamper your independence. For example, you may have to ask for help in brushing your hair or emptying your catheter. You may need help in reaching dishes on a shelf or getting in or out of the car. You may need help carrying a tray in the cafeteria. You may need extra time changing classrooms at school.

Take a few minutes to think about your specific needs. Ask yourself:

- What does independence mean to me?
- How independent am I in my different activities at home, at school, in my extracurricular life?

- What things get in the way of my being as independent as I would like to be?
- How can I deal with the obstacles in my way? Is there any way to get over, around, or under them? Do I need help to do so?

Asking yourself these questions—and considering the answers—is an important step toward taking control of your life.

The next step is to think of someone with whom you feel comfortable sharing your thoughts and feelings. This might be a friend, a parent, a favorite aunt, uncle, or cousin, a teacher, a minister, or a therapist. See if he or she can think of any ways you can overcome these barriers. Sometimes it helps to "brainstorm" an idea with others. Just let ideas roll out without any limitations. Some may be truly absurd! Some may be wonderful!

Problem   You are a whiz at science and want to be a theoretical physicist. You see that an obstacle to reaching your goal might be that you are not able to speak clearly. How are you going to communicate?

Ideas   You and your fellow brainstormer might come up with several ideas that could help you communicate more effectively. One might be a voice synthesizer which speaks your choice of words. Or you could communicate in writing via a computer. You may also want to investigate more speech therapy to see if you can improve the way you speak.
Or:
Perhaps you know a young adult who has a disability similar to yours. This person has probably had many experiences like yours. Ask this person for any ideas or suggestions that would be helpful to you. If you don't know anyone you could talk with, try contacting a disability organization such as United Cerebral Palsy, the Spina Bifida Association of America, or one of the others listed in the back of the book. Someone there might be able to help you find a sympathetic ear. In New York City, for example,

there is a group called the Networking Project for Disabled Women and Girls, sponsored by the YWCA on Lexington Avenue. Through this project, women with physical disabilities serve as mentors for high school girls with physical disabilities. They talk about employment, relationships with parents, sexuality, and socialization. Sometimes the mentors and their high school proteges go out to lunch or to a movie.

Remember: Independence is like a coin with two sides. One side includes freedom and making decisions for yourself. The other side says "Responsibility." What does that mean? It means that you do not live in a vacuum; you are not a Lone Ranger. You have to be responsible for the way you act and the decisions you make . . . for how your actions affect the lives of those around you.

Read on! The next chapters suggest more specific strategies for maneuvering around roadblocks to independence.

CHAPTER 11

How Do You Balance Your Strengths and Challenges?

▼ ▼ ▼ ▼ ▼ ▼ ▼ ▼ ▼ ▼ ▼ ▼ ▼ ▼ ▼ ▼

Being able to pinpoint your strengths is important in setting goals for:

- work
- education
- training
- hobbies and leisure activities
- relationships
- and even where you want to live

And setting honest and realistic goals is essential to your independence. What if your goal is to be a surgeon? If you got a D in biology and can't stand the sight of blood, that may not be a realistic goal. But if you enjoyed dissecting in biology class and are curious about how the body works, it may be a suitable goal. Even if you use a wheelchair, your goal may be a real possibility, thanks to current and future technological advances.

▼ Your Strengths

Defining your strengths and abilities is a big step. It is also an important step, because sometimes you can use your strengths to overcome obstacles that stand between you and your goals. For example, perhaps it is too exhausting for you to commute to an office job every day. But if you have good computer skills, you may be able to figure out a way to work at home and "commute" to work via a modem.

Here is how the teenagers interviewed responded when we asked:

What are your strengths?

John: I'm very positive about what I'm doing in my life and don't let my disability stop me usually.

April: Talking, cooking, spelling, giving advice, and doing hair are my strengths.

Glen: I'm a good leader and creative in projects. I'm humorous and have original ideas.

Tiffany: I am happy and kind to others, to friends. I do want to do well. I feel good about myself.

Tim: I work hard. I don't give up.

Alyssa: I'm good at helping people with their problems. I'm determined and strong and make my own decisions. I'm not going to be unhappy to make someone else happy.

Edward: I care. I am nice. I have a good personality once you get to know me.

Timeka: I'm independent and try to do things I'm not supposed to be doing—things others don't except me to do.

Sam: My ears are pretty good and my arms are strong.

June: I do well in school because I have a good brain.

Myla: I can sing very well. I am good at being able to deal with my disability. I can also figure out my abilities, the things I can do well.

Art: Weight lifting, swimming, and computer games are my strong points.

Nicole: I can be patient and I can be thoughtful, attractive, pleasant, humorous, reliable, responsible, courteous.

Tina: I make good grades. My talents include cross-stitch, sewing, crochet, and art work.

The personal resources mentioned above fit into several categories:

- Physical Abilities: What you do well to overcome the physical limitations of your disability
- Mental Abilities: What intellectual abilities allow you to achieve and enjoy yourself through learning
- Personal Qualities: What character strengths and values give you personal strength
- Interpersonal Abilities: What abilities you have to reach out to others, to work with and to help them
- Specific skills and talents: What technical, artistic, domestic, or practical skills or talents you have mastered

You may have abilities in one of these areas or in more than one. Or your abilities might be found in entirely different realms. The chart on the next two pages may help you evaluate your strengths. As you read through the skills listed, ask yourself which of these skills you have, and which you would like to have.

If you have trouble figuring out your strengths for yourself, ask your parents, a brother or sister, a teacher or counselor, or a friend what they think your personal assets are. Do they match your ideas? If they are different, list them in two columns, one marked "My Ideas" and the other, "Other's Ideas." You might discover that others have uncovered "gold" you never knew you had!

▼ Your Challenges

Many of the obstacles to achieving your goals lie within you. Sometimes these are parts of you that can be changed, if you work on them. For instance, you may want to work on being more patient with people who don't think or react as quickly as you do. Or you may realize that you need to spend more time listening to others' ideas instead of always talking about your own ideas. There might also be changes you'd like to make to your life to enrich it, by cultivating new hobbies or interests. Although Part 1 touched on the subject of personal limitations, it's important to look at these challenges again. You need to recognize whether they will be roadblocks to reaching goals, and if they will, to think about how you can deal with them. In taking stock of what you are missing,

STRENGTHS

Mental Abilities

- Writing
- Reading
- Mathematics
- Foreign language skills
- Problem solving
- Complex thinking
  (ability to see a situation from many perspectives; to see the shades of gray between black and white)
- Abstract thinking
  (ability to see patterns and relationships; to see broad, overarching categories)
- Planning
- Understanding
- Teaching
- Computer skills
- Memory
- Other

Physical Abilities (General Abilities)

- Stamina/endurance
- Tolerance of pain
- Dexterity
- Upper body/lower body strength
- Quick reflexes
- Flexibility
- Eye-hand coordination
- Overall coordination of body
- Balance

Abilities in Specific Sports (with or without wheelchair or assistive device)

- Basketball
- Baseball
- Football
- Tennis
- Swimming
- Track and field
- Weight lifting
- Aerobics
- Dancing
- Rugby
- Lacrosse
- Skiing (Downhill/Cross-country)
- Kayaking
- Sailing
- Fishing
- Volleyball
- Racquetball
- Hiking
- Mountain climbing
- Flying a plane
- Riflery
- Archery
- Other

STRENGTHS

Personal Qualities

- Honest
- Dependable
- Sense of humor
- Caring
- Thoughtful
- Responsible
- Charitable
- Gentle
- Kind
- Self-confident
- Accepting of others
- Organized
- Patient
- Even-tempered
- Fun to be with
- Up-beat personality
- Other

Interpersonal Abilities

- Listening to others
- Sharing feelings with others
- Standing up for yourself
- Seeing where help is needed
- Putting others at ease
- Tactfulness
- Persuasiveness
- Comforting others
- Giving your time
- Giving your talent
- Giving your money
- Other

Specific Skills and Talents

- Woodworking
- Music (instrument, vocal, composing)
- Needlework
- Sewing
- Knitting
- Cross stitch
- Embroidery
- Gardening
- Raising pets
- Computer games
- Collecting
- Telephoning
- Rocketry
- Photography
- Ham radio operating
- Model building
- Jewelry making
- Art
- Painting
- Sculpting
- Cartooning
- Calligraphy
- Chess
- Auto mechanics
- Other

you can then decide: whether you want to change in order to meet your goals; and if so, how you can do that.

What things about yourself do you want to work on?

John: I need to overcome my shyness. I also need to improve my physical strength and improve my speech some more.

April: I'm learning to be mature, to get out on my own more. I also want to get taller!

Glen: I like myself the way I am.

Tiffany: I would like to be able to talk and walk better. I'd like to get a job, drive, and have a boyfriend.

Tim: I should be talking more often.

Alyssa: I need to work on my anger. I get a big attitude and my friends know I'm mad. My bad moods give me an attitude and I take it out on everyone else, even though it's not their fault.

Edward: I should be more outgoing and talk to people. I should take the first step sometimes.

Timeka: I need to work on accomplishing goals to go on to college and into a career.

Sam: My legs.

June: The usual—guys! I want to work on being in crowds and around guys.

Myla: I want to be able to walk better.

Art: Can't think of anything.

Nicole: I might be able to open up to people more. For example, I don't tell people if my feelings are hurt.

Al: My attitude. I need to improve, to accept more responsibility, and not be so lazy with a capital L.

Tina: Independence!

Obviously, personal limitations, like strengths, can be grouped into categories. These include:

- Social Abilities: the need to learn to respond to others more freely, to extend a hand first, to relate to others more positively
- Physical Abilities: the need to improve or develop new strength or skills in your body
- Personal Development: the need to improve your personality and attitude toward yourself and others.
- OK where I am: the feeling that there is no great need or urge to change.

As you did in taking stock of your strengths, now identify your challenges or weaknesses. Which of the abilities listed on page 100 do you need to work on?

Again, if you have trouble figuring this out, talk with someone with whom you are comfortable. Make sure you really want to know what you need to work on. Assure the person you talk to that you are sincere and that your feelings won't be hurt if he or she is honest.

▼ Balancing Strengths and Challenges

After you've listed the areas where you need improvement, take another look at your strengths. Is there any relationship between your strengths and challenges? For example, is a particular weak point preventing you from making the most of a strong point?

Edward, for instance, says his strengths are caring, being nice, and having a good personality. His weakness, he says, is that he is not outgoing and doesn't talk much to others.

Problem   How are people going to know what a caring, nice guy Edward is if he doesn't talk with them?

Idea   In order to bring out his strengths, Edward might want to work on communicating with others. This is not always easy for someone who is shy. But it can be done through practice with friends and family! It might also be helpful to get some assertiveness training with a psychologist or counselor. (Assertiveness means talking for yourself without attacking others. For more on this, see Chapter 14.) Edward could also go to the library and look for books that deal with speaking up. They would likely be listed under "communications" or "assertiveness" in the card catalog. He might also look under "psychology" in the card catalog

CHALLENGES

Social

- Relating to others
- Being at ease with others
- Introducing yourself and others
- Making others feel welcome
- Making others feel comfortable
- Carrying on a conversation
- Listening to others
- Helping others
- Sharing feelings
- Being dependable
- Standing up for yourself
- Taking on responsibility
- Seeing others' viewpoints
- Asking for help when necessary
- Other . . .

Physical

- Watching weight
- Exercising
- Strengthening
- Keeping in shape
- Not over-doing
- Personal hygiene
- Healthy diet
- Sticking to medical schedule (injections, pills if needed)
- Other . . .

Personal Development

- Having a sense of who you are
- Feeling good about yourself
- Forgiving yourself when necessary
- Accepting yourself
- Allowing yourself to be who you are
- Taking risks
- Taking care of yourself
- Taking responsibility
- Sticking to your principles
- Setting realistic goals
- Other . . .

or under that heading in a book store. There are many good new paperback books on communication.

Problem Alyssa has trouble dealing with anger. She gets into a funky mood and takes it out on everyone else—even though it's not anyone else's fault.

Idea Alyssa's strength is listening to others. She helps them solve their problems. Maybe it's time she took that skill and used it for herself. She could "listen" to herself—either by listening to her own thoughts, by writing a "letter" to herself, or by tape recording herself. Or she might want to talk with someone she trusts about why she's feeling angry. That way she'll get her anger out, which is necessary, and not let it interfere with her relationships with her friends.

Problem You might want to change something about yourself that you cannot change. For instance, you may exercise and exercise, but you just can't build up the muscles in your legs as much as you'd like. Or you may have a good singing voice but your lungs may not be strong enough to support sustained singing. So a singing career is not possible.

Beyond the Brick Wall Sometimes there are real limits to what you can change. It's time, then, to pause, and to say to yourself that you have tried as hard as you can. You can't do any more. You've hit a brick wall. It's time to make another decision: Stop spending so much energy in that area. Maybe instead of walking, you'll need to use a wheelchair. Or you may need to use a speaking device to communicate. Or you'll need to use braces and crutches. You'll need to mourn your loss of the dream to walk, to talk, or to walk without assistive devices. That's hard. But once you've done it . . . you'll find that there is more than one way to get around or to talk (some boring, uncreative people assume walking and talking can only be done in certain ways!). You'll also find you have energy to try new ways of doing things that help you reach your goal: being independent in whatever ways you can be. For example. . . .

Problem   You have always dreamed of not having a disability. You want to play shortstop for the Red Sox. You work hard in physical therapy and with your exercise equipment at home. But you cannot build up the strength you need in your legs.

Idea   You have an understanding and knowledge of baseball. You have a good voice and you write well. What about aiming toward a career as a baseball announcer? or a sports reporter? To see if you would enjoy this kind of job, you could volunteer to be a statistician for your high school sports teams. Or become a sports writer for the school paper.

CHAPTER 12

WHEN CAN'T YOU DO IT ALONE?

▼ ▼ ▼ ▼ ▼ ▼ ▼ ▼ ▼ ▼ ▼

As the last two chapters pointed out, most teenagers have a mix of strengths and weaknesses. Often, your disability may have little or nothing to do with what you can and cannot do. For example, you might have had a green thumb or a knack for foreign languages whether or not you had a disability. Then again, your disability might have a great deal to do with your abilities in a particular area. For example, you might be able to type 90 words per minute because you've been communicating via a computer most of your life. Or you may know a lot about hospitals because you have been in them so often.

Sometimes when your disability presents real challenges, there are ways around them. Other times, as mentioned in the last chapter, you run up against a brick wall. No matter how hard you try, you just can't manage on your own. When your personal brick wall is something that

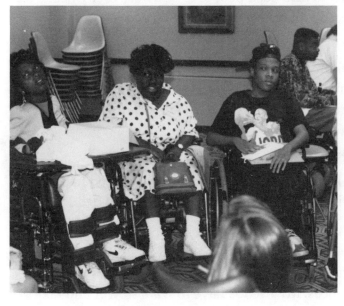

you *want* to, but don't *need* to do, the disappointment can be overwhelming. But as Chapter 12 discusses, you can often come up with an alternate goal that is equally satisfying. When your personal brick wall is something that you *need* to do, however, it is a different story. For example, if you are unable to feed yourself or wash your hair, you are still going to have to accomplish these things somehow. Usually, the solution is to ask for help.

This chapter looks at some of the reasons it is sometimes essential to get help when you have a physical disability. It then suggests ways to assess whether you truly can or cannot do something. Finally, it offers strategies to help you decide whether you need help, and if so, how much.

To get a feel for the kinds of physical limitations that can be related to disabilities, we asked:

What is your disability?

Do you have special needs?

John: I have cerebral palsy and speech and learning disabilities. I'm having trouble controlling my balance. So I have special needs every day.

April: I have spina bifida. I need bars in the bathtub and I can't drive.

Glen: I have osteogenesis imperfecta. Sometimes I need to leave classes early to get through the halls to my next class. I can't walk long distances or stand for a long time. I have limited speed even in the wheelchair. Sometimes I need more help, especially when I break a leg, like I did a year and a half ago. I also need people to be aware of my needs for accessibility.

Tiffany: I have cerebral palsy and a speech disability. I have special needs in dressing, combing my hair, and eating every day. I am trying out language machines that will talk for me. I use sign language.

Tim: I have muscular dystrophy. I need ramps and elevators for my wheelchair. I also need help showering, dressing, and getting into bed.

Alyssa: I have osteogenesis imperfecta. My friend helps put the wheelchair that I use at school in the car at school. I also have trouble walking long distances. My friends have to walk slower and take stops for me.

Edward: I have muscular dystrophy. I have people move me around, take me places, get my clothes, and help me dress. I need help lots of the time.

Timeka: My disability is spina bifida. I use a wheelchair and I need my things for work and my personal supplies placed so that I can reach them. I need help getting clothes out of the closet and off the hanger.

Sam: I have cerebral palsy, a learning disability, a vision impairment, and epilepsy. Sometimes I use a walker and sometimes a wheelchair. I need help getting food and drink, and putting on my braces. I have limits in walking and writing.

June: I have cerebral palsy. I know I have some limitations, but in my mind I say I can do anything.

Myla: I have spina bifida. I need help reaching things from high shelves, as I'm short. I need help getting my shoes on sometimes.

Art: I have spina bifida. Don't need any help I can think of.

Nicole: I have cerebral palsy. I need help regularly to move from one chair to another. But I'm not limited in the future in my education, career, and family.

Al: I have spina bifida. I need special accommodations for a wheelchair, especially when traveling. Sometimes I can't reach things because I'm not tall enough. I need help about 50 percent of the time.

Tina: I have muscular dystrophy. I need help daily. I have limitations in running and in school work. I have a "Canine Companion" dog, a golden retriever. He goes with me to school and everywhere, and also opens doors and picks up things for me. I had two weeks of training with him in New York. He attracts attention; sometimes I

compete with him for attention. I've had him for a
year.

These teenagers assess the specific needs arising from their disabilities in practical terms—they look at the ways their disabilities affect
their lives. You may think of other ways disability enters your life. Some
of you may need special bowel or bladder care; some girls may need help
during their menstrual cycle; some may need to delay toileting when
there is no accessible bathroom available. Bathing and other types of personal care may be concerns as well.

In working toward independence, it is important to factor in your disability. You need to take into account the ways it affects your life and the
time and effort your special needs require. You also need to recognize the
need to ask for help at times. . . .

▼ Asking for Help

Growing up involves learning to do all those things you haven't yet
mastered in order to become that independent person you want to be.
Perhaps you think that independence means you can do everything by
and for yourself. But, in fact, one of the most important things adults
come to know is that they can't always do things for themselves. Sometimes they need to ask for help. This is the sign of a truly mature person:
knowing when you can do something for yourself and when you need to
accept help. So:

**How do you
decide if
something
is too hard
to do?**

John: I don't know. It may depend on the kind of
mood I'm in.

April: I try it awhile; if I can't do it, I decide it's too
hard.

Glen: If I see stairs, I know it's too much. I can
handle one step, but no more.

Tim: I try it. If I can't do it, I stop.

Alyssa: It's too hard if I flat out can't do it.

Edward: If I can't do it, I keep trying.

Timeka: I experience it and see if I can. I don't like to give up.

Sam: I look at it.

June: I give everything a shot unless I know it's impossible. For example, I went on a field trip with a bunch of teens. The guys wanted me to climb a thirty-five-foot ladder, get harnessed into a trapeze, and swing across. I told them, "No! That's impossible!" But going to Europe last summer with my class was not impossible.

Myla: My disability is my only limitation. Like I can't do things or go places with my friends. I can't climb some things; climbing ladders is hard.

Art: I can tell just by looking at it.

Nicole: If it hurts or is too frustrating, I say so.

Al: Sometimes I don't know something is too difficult until it's too late, so I mess up at work—at Dad's office, for example.

Tina: I try it out.

You, too, may use several methods to determine whether you can do something or whether it is going to be too difficult:

- Trial and error: Attempting to do a job to see if, in fact, you can accomplish the task.
- Sizing up: Remembering things you have been able to do in the past and comparing those tasks to the present task.
- Trying once more: Even if you haven't been able to do something in the past, challenging yourself to try it again.

In deciding how much effort you are going to put into something, you might want to think about:

How important is this to do? For example, when you do things yourself it may take two hours to get out of bed, bathe or shower, dress, brush your hair, eat breakfast, and get out to the school bus stop by 7:00 a.m. This means a 5:00 a.m. wake-up call. If your Mom helps you, it takes an hour and means a 6:00 a.m. arising. Either decision is fine. It depends on how important it is to you to be able to do this yourself. Do you need to do this for yourself to show yourself you can? If you don't do it yourself will you feel guilty or as if you are imposing too much on your mother? Maybe you and your folks should share your feelings about the time and effort needed. *Do* they mind getting up early to help you? Do you (or they) realistically think you can improve your skills and cut your time through practice? In the end, if you feel better when you do something without any help, do it that way! But if you are happy to have help, then go that route.

   Are there alternative ways to accomplish a goal? If you are unable to do something such as dressing yourself, don't give up. There are all sorts of tools and aids that can help. There are catalogs full of orthopedic supplies and aids to help you be physically independent: zipper-pullers, button hookers, and specially designed fashionable clothes that are easier to put on, for example. Contact physical and occupational therapists, rehabilitation departments of hospitals, or your doctor for suppliers of these tools. Also see the back of this book for information on some books listing sources of tools and aids.

   Another example of a creative source of help is Tina's "Canine Companion," the dog who helps her open doors and pick up things from the floor. Several organizations that train support dogs are listed in the back of the book.

   Remember to use friends, family, and professionals to help you find ways to become as independent as you can be.

Problem   If you need a lot of help because of your disability, how can you still be independent?

Idea   Think of yourself as one of those big executives who runs a conglomerate. The executive makes decisions and others execute them for him. He is independent; he is making the decisions and deciding they will be carried out. He is thoughtful and considerate of those who work for him. *You* are the executive of your life! It doesn't matter if you actually do the driving or comb your hair. *You* make the decisions regarding when and how those things are done in your life!

Some of you may find that you tire easily or that you often feel pain. You need help then. That's OK. You're learning the very mature way of dealing with life: sometimes you ask for help. You are not being lazy by saying that you cannot brush your own hair today. On the days when you feel energetic and pain-free, you do your own hair. Learning when to be dependent and when to be independent—and that each is OK—is learning to be *interdependent*.

One of the hardest things to deal with is not being able to do something you were able to do yesterday. This happens with some disabilities. It is hard to deal with loss. You may feel disappointed, angry, depressed, listless, or scared. These feelings are real and legitimate. They are not crazy. You need to recognize them and deal with them.

When feelings of hurt, anger, or loss are kept inside, they seem to grow and expand. Pretty soon it seems like you're carrying around a heavy sack on your shoulders. You feel weighted down. You may lose sleep, have no desire to eat. Or you may find it difficult to concentrate. You may shut yourself in your room more and more.

Key It is important not to bottle up your feelings within yourself. Find someone to share your feelings with. It might be a good idea to find a counselor, psychologist, social worker, or pastor to talk with. Whoever you work with will be able to help you sort through your feelings. He or she will help you find ways to label your feelings and then help you to deal with them.

Decision Point

Tyrone felt alone and scared. He had recently learned that he would have to use a wheelchair instead of crutches. The doctor had told him that he was having an exacerbation of his muscular dystrophy. He was sad and angry and anxious. He felt that there was no one who would understand what he was going through. He wanted to tell his mother, but his mother was over-burdened as it was, with her 9 to 5 job and six kids. How could Tyrone add another worry to his mom's load?

(Continued)

Day after day, Tyrone kept his feelings to himself, and each day he felt more isolated and energyless. He had always been a B student; now his grades started to drop. He had trouble sleeping and didn't like to eat. He found it difficult to concentrate; he shut himself in his room more and more. Then one day, Mr. Samuelson, his history teacher, kept him after class. Mr. Samuelson told him that he was concerned and that he felt Tyrone should talk with someone who could help him. He said he would help Tyrone make an appointment with a school counselor.

Tyrone talked with the counselor. He felt relieved when the counselor listened and told him that his feelings were understandable and OK. He was going through a period of loss; it took strength to deal with what he had to face. What was not OK, said the counselor, was to assume that Tyrone had to work through this by himself. Tyrone began to feel more energetic and had more interest in his classes. When he felt "down," he no longer kept it inside. Instead, he made an appointment to talk with the counselor.

▼ Dealing with Offers of Help

When you have a physical disability, you may receive frequent offers of help from family, friends, and even strangers. Sometimes you can use the help, but many times you would rather do it yourself.

What do you do if someone tries to help you and you don't need help?

John: I just say politely, "I don't need your help. Please don't take it the wrong way, but I can do this on my own. Thank you."

April: I go along with it or say, "No, thank you."

Glen: To make them feel good, I go along with it. I might say "I've got it" first, but if they persist I let them go ahead.

Tiffany: I refuse; no help needed.

Tim: I let them help me.

Alyssa: I tell them I can do it.

Edward: I explain I don't need the help. I do not like to be rude.

Timeka: I say, "It's OK. I can do it."

Sam: I just ignore the help and do it myself.

June: "No thanks. It's all right. I've got it."

Myla: I usually tell them, "I have it. Leave me alone."

Art: I just let them help. Anyway, I get lazy sometimes.

Nicole: I very politely say, "Please don't help me. I think I can do it myself. I'd like to try it myself. But if I can't, I know you're around to help."

Al: It all depends on my mood. I could be grouchy and say "No" or I could say "No thank you," or I might say "No thank you" sarcastically.

Tina: I tell them I do not need help in this, but thanks.

There are a variety of ways to respond to others' offers of help. Some people do not want to offend others, so accept offers of help even when they do not want or need it. Others reject all offers of help. Then others, like Nicole, stress their needs to do the task by themselves, but then accept the offer if it's absolutely needed. Al also brings in another dimension, which is how your feelings help you decide if or how you can accept help.

Remember that it is your *choice* when, if, or how you accept help. It might help you to make a study of the circumstances in which you can take help or reject it. Are there certain people from whom you don't like to accept help? Are there others whose feelings you don't like to hurt so you always accept their offers? Are there still others whose offers you feel OK either accepting or rejecting? It's OK to feel that you can accept or reject help from different people. Who you accept help from is your choice.

Idea   A light touch is always a good bridge to explain to others
how you feel. Think of some funny way to turn down help
if you don't want it. You think of your own bridge of
humor. You have your own special way of expressing
yourself, so the design of your bridge will be yours alone.
It's helpful to think about what you want to say ahead of
time so you're prepared. . . .

CHAPTER 13

WHOSE EXPECTATIONS?

▼ ▼ ▼ ▼ ▼ ▼ ▼ ▼ ▼ ▼ ▼ ▼ ▼

Expectations are important. They provide a framework for anticipating the future, whether it be in the next few moments or ten years from now. Expectations help you set goals. They help you map your plans for the future.

Expectations can be for success or failure. Sometimes they are based on past experiences. For instance, if you have had lots of successes, you will be more likely to think you are going to succeed in the future. On the other hand, if you have had lots of failures, you may be less likely to think of yourself succeeding. However, most of you will have had a mixture of triumphs and defeats. This is what most people experience.

Expectations come from within yourself and from others. Sometimes the expectations that you or others have for yourself are unreasonably high. Sometimes they are too low. When your expectations differ from other people's expectations, either you or those around you will be disappointed. There may be feelings of discontent and conflict, either within yourself or with those around you. To find out how common these kinds of conflicts are, we asked:

Do you ever think others expect too little of you?

Edward: Yes. In DVR [Department of Vocational Rehabilitation], they read reports and listen to the experts, not to me. So you have to protect yourself. It really annoys me.

Timeka: Sometimes.

Sam: Yes, sometimes.

June: Everybody does.

Nicole: No. But at the high school where classes for kids with orthopedic disabilities are held, they treated us too immaturely and did everything for us. I didn't want a double standard, so I chose to attend my home high school.

Art: Yes. Sometimes at my Dad's office they won't let me type or use the computer. I just take messages and do things like that.

Tina: No.

What kind of expectations do you have of yourself? What kind of expectations do your parents, teachers, and others have of you? Are they the same or different?

▼ When Expectations Differ

If your expectations and those of others are alike, you probably feel pretty comfortable working toward your goals. But what if your expectations and the expectations of family, friends, or teachers are very different? How do you deal with this difference?

Let's first look at a situation in which someone has set standards or expectations that are too low for you.

Example Mrs. Jones, your English teacher, has given your class an essay to write. Most of your classmates have lots of red marks and suggestions on their papers when they are returned. Yours has few corrections (even though you dashed it off while watching a video). Plus, the teacher has written in the margin: "I admire you for trying so hard." After class, you tell Mrs. Jones you would like to know how you can do better. She pats you on the head, and says you are "so brave to deal with the wheelchair!"

How do you respond?

- Do you agree with her? *Are* you very brave to deal with being in a wheelchair? Should you receive extra points for dealing with this situation (even though you spent thirty minutes dashing off the essay while concentrating on a video)?
- Do you feel angry that she sees your disability as defining you—limiting you? If you feel that way, how do you tell

Mrs. Jones that you want to be judged like all the rest of the students?
- Can you think of another response?

There are situations where just the opposite of the experience above occurs, where someone has expectations of you that are not always realistic or good for you.

Example You are usually happy and up-beat around family and friends. However, there are times when you feel frustrated and angry and sad. Your family responds to these feelings with "That's not the kid we know and love" as if those feelings are not legitimate and part of anyone's real bag of feelings.

How do you respond?

- Do you tell yourself that your family and friends do so much for you that the least you can do for them is to hold in your feelings and not burden them with your sadness or anger?
- Do you realize that you have a right to your feelings? That it is normal to have down times and up times and in-between times? Do you tell your family and friends that these feelings are a part of you and that you need to share them?
- What other response can you think of?

There are times when expectations are just different. For instance, parents and therapists may have different expectations than you do about what you can achieve physically, either more or less than what you think you can do. Ask them: "Why do you think I can/cannot achieve this?"

- Have tests shown that you have/don't have the necessary strength?
- Is it unusual for someone with spina bifida to be able to do this particular exercise?

- Do your parents expect a miracle to occur so that you will walk?

Knowing the reasons for their expectations will help you ground your own personal expectations in reality. This information will help you avoid situations in which you feel you have to achieve the "impossible." For example, you have been lifting weights in physical therapy to strengthen arm muscles. Your therapist adds five more pounds. You try to lift the weights. You try again. You can't budge them. You would really like to lift them, but you feel you've found your Brick Wall. At this point, it's very important to find out if the therapist knows something you don't know that would convince you to keep trying. Or is your gut instinct right? Should you insist on stopping?

Challenging others' expectations can also help you avoid situations in which you feel you must mask your real abilities. "You're tired," says Mom after you leave therapy, even though you're feeling full of energy. "No, no, don't hide it." It's as if she knows how you feel better than you do. If you keep quiet because you don't feel like confronting her, it can lead to a complete misunderstanding on Mom's part. She may worry about you or baby you when there is really no need. You can do yourself and your mother a favor by letting her know what your real energy level is.

These "mismatch" situations (times when your abilities do not match your own or others' expectations) can create physical and psychological stress and anxiety. But when you have your own basis for determining what you can expect from yourself, you will then be able to let family, friends, or professionals know what your limits and horizons are. Sometimes others will not be able to give up unrealistically high/low expectations for you. It's then time to say to yourself, "That is their problem. I know my abilities and disabilities and will do what I know I can."

CHAPTER 14

Do You Speak Up for Yourself?

▼ ▼ ▼ ▼ ▼ ▼ ▼ ▼ ▼ ▼ ▼

Once you have inventoried what independence means to you; what your assets are and what you need to work on; decided when and how you want to accept or reject help from others; thought about deciding when expectations are appropriate or not—then it's time to move on to another important part of becoming the person you want to be: speaking for yourself.

Speaking for yourself is called assertiveness. Speaking up is sometimes easier for those who are extroverts or outgoing. Often it is harder for people who are introverted or shy. But everyone can learn to speak for him or herself!

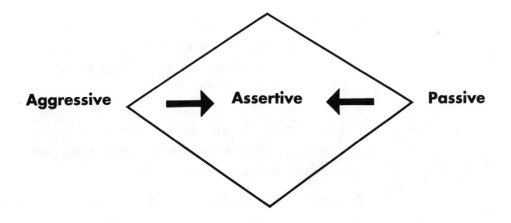

Aggressive ⟶ **Assertive** ⟵ **Passive**

Assertiveness falls between aggressiveness and passiveness. Aggressive people seldom think of the rights or needs of others; they tend to think only of themselves. Passive people tend to think only of others and do not tend to their own rights and needs. It's important to *balance* your own needs and the needs of others. Assertiveness means you can express your own needs, but not at the expense of others.

The teenagers we interviewed vary in the comfort they feel in speaking up for themselves, the frequency they speak up for themselves, and the situations in which they do speak for themselves. We asked them:

Do you speak up for yourself?

Do you feel OK speaking up for yourself?

John: Mostly. Yes.

April: Sometimes, mostly at home. I guess I feel OK about it.

Glen: Somewhat. Sometimes. When I was little, I put others ahead of me. I still do. But now I speak up for myself when it's very important. I feel OK if it's not in front of a million people.

Tim: Sometimes. If I get stuck in my wheelchair I speak up for myself. I feel OK about that.

Alyssa: Yes. When I don't agree, I say I don't and why. If I don't speak up for myself, no one else is going to.

Edward: No, not really. Sometimes I speak up for myself with my family; never with strangers unless I get real mad. I only speak up when others are mean to me or do something that throws me, like when you ask someone in a store to do something and they turn away. I'd rather do it for myself, because sometimes others speak for you and they say something you don't want them to say.

Timeka: Yes, in the majority of cases. I feel OK about speaking up for myself.

Sam: Yes, except when I have seizures. Yes, I feel OK about speaking up for myself. I can defend myself. I have ways.

June: Yes, I speak up for myself in all situations. If I don't do it, I'll end up with something I don't want.

Myla: Yes, I speak up for myself when people are trying to help me and I don't need help.

Art: All the time! I do it when I'm getting into a fight or argument to show that I'm a person, not anything else. I can stick up for myself.

Nicole: Yes, especially when my feelings are hurt, or I'm angry, or something is wrong—like unfairness because of my disability. There is no such thing as a designated advocate. You have to advocate for yourself.

Al: Yes, in most situations.

Tina: Yes, in all situations.

Sometimes people hesitate to speak up for themselves because they worry about what others will think. What if they come across as being rude, pushy, whiny, or arrogant? Usually, however, this is not what happens. The teenagers we interviewed described mostly positive reactions when we asked:

How do others react when you speak up for yourself?

John: I think they respect me for that.

April: Surprised, happy.

Glen: They're fine about it. No one has ever refused to do what I said.

Tim: They are glad to help.

Alyssa: My parents usually get mad. Last year the principal called my parents because a guy talking with my friends and me had a weapon. The principal doesn't like my friends (some of them use drugs, although I don't). I told him that the "parking lot people" (cheerleaders, popular kids) also use drugs but nobody gets to them. It's wrong to tab people by the way they look. I said so to the principal and my parents got mad at me.

Timeka: People are OK about it. Sometimes they argue with my viewpoint.

Sam: They accept it and respect me.

June: Some people think I speak up just because I am so worried that someone will do something for me.

Myla: Some of them are amazed! Some look like they're frightened if I say something they don't understand.

Art: Surprised! Very surprised.

Nicole: Surprised. They most often respect me. They may temporarily resent me, but later, they respect me.

Al: Usually positive. It gets respect.

Tina: They feel good that I do. They respect me.

▼ Why Assert Yourself?

Whether or not you are encouraged to be assertive, there are many good reasons to speak up. These include:

To show that you can stand up for yourself: It's important to speak for yourself so that you can start working toward becoming an individual, separate from those around you. Sometimes it is more important to do so if you have a disability because people tend to make decisions or to speak for you. Edward has stated this quite clearly in his experiences. Relying on others to speak for you may be the result of spending so much time in the medical system, where doctors and other professionals make so many decisions about your care.

To ensure that you get what you want: As June points out, you may need to speak up for yourself so you won't end up with something you don't want. Sometimes others assume that if you have a physical disability, you may not be able to make a decision for yourself, or that somehow you are not as smart or capable as others. You may also spend lots of time with various doctors and therapists who have many ideas about what is best for you. Do you always follow their advice or do you think about what they've said, evaluate it, and then make your own decision? Remember Robert's experience in

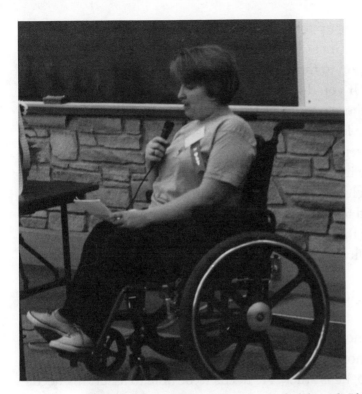

deciding whether or not he would have surgery (page 44). He weighed the outcome of the surgery against his desire to start college soon. He and his parents talked about his options, and then he made his decision. There are instances, however, when you don't have a choice, such as in life-threatening situations.

To assert your independence: Parents and teenagers are going to have differences of opinions. This is part of growing into adulthood. If you have to physically rely on your parents for help, it's a more difficult struggle. It's tough to say "No!" to a parent who has just lugged your wheelchair out of the car trunk. But you do not have to go along with everything they say just because they sometimes help you.

To ensure that you are heard: As Alyssa says, "If I don't (speak up for myself) no one else is going to." When you were a child, your parents talked with teachers and doctors about what would be going on in your life. But now that you're older, it's time to try on your wings—to speak for yourself so that what you think and feel is heard. For instance, you may want physical therapy twice a week instead of three times so that you can join the ceramics club at school. Let your parents and therapists know how important this is to you and that you'll exercise on your own for thirty minutes that evening.

To make sure your feelings are understood: Nicole explains how important it is to speak for yourself and to explain the unfairness of situations that you sometimes encounter because of your disability. For instance, you may find that your brand new school, reputed to be barrier free, has steps up to the auditorium and a dangerously steep ramp into a side entrance. Allow yourself to express your feelings of anger and frustration to those who allowed the building to be constructed this way. If you do not feel comfortable expressing your feelings in person to these people, share them with a friend or a parent. Then either write a letter or make a phone call to those responsible. It is important to describe the violation of building covenants and codes. It is equally important for you to express your feelings of anger, of being excluded, of having to deal with a dangerous situation. Officials need to hear the personal hurt attached to the disregard of the law. (Check the Appendix for more information on laws and building accessibility.)

To assure physical safety: Surely the basic need of everyone is for personal safety. Tim says he speaks for himself when he gets stuck in his wheelchair. When he finds himself in this situation, he needs to be able to tell others how to get him going again. If he can't explain to others how to help, he is stuck. He needs to be able to assert his needs in order to be independent.

Sometimes you may need to speak up not to request help, but to refuse it. Sometimes what others see as helping you may actually hurt you. For instance, you may have a certain way of climbing stairs with your crutches. A stranger comes along and sees you straining to climb to the next step. He grabs your arm when you are not balanced. This can be physically dangerous. You need to be able to tell this well-intentioned person to let you climb the steps by yourself in your own way.

When you are physically vulnerable in a situation, it is important for you to take control. In the two instances described above, that ability would protect you from danger.

To speak up when you are not being treated with respect: Both Nicole and Edward say they need to feel angry before they can speak up for themselves. But you have the right to speak up at other times than just when you are angry. Anger is a great energizer to action— but you need to be able to speak up without being angry as well.

If you can see that the problem is the other person's (even though it affects you), it often helps if you can react in a more thoughtful, detached way. For example, have you ever met someone who sees you as a young child just because you use a wheelchair? Someone who pats you on the head or speaks in that grown-up-to-young-child voice, higher pitched and louder? Try to see the problem as being the other person's; retain *your* self-dignity. Speak maturely and calmly, letting the person know that you are not a child.

Now take a look at yourself. Ask yourself the following questions:

- Do you assert yourself?
- How do you assert yourself?
- Do you assert yourself in certain situations?
- Can you assert yourself with certain people, and not with others?
- Can you assert yourself at home and not in public?
- Or out in public but not with your parents?
- Does it feel OK to speak for yourself when it comes to disability issues but not while out on a date?

Decision Point

Brendon was feeling nervous and on edge. The prom was three weeks off. The whole school was wrapped up in the preparations and discussions about who was asking whom to go. Brendon was well known in the school and served on the student council. Although he did lots of things with his gang of friends, he had never asked a girl for a date. He wondered how a girl would react. He was smart and looked OK, but he wondered if he would be rejected because he wore braces and used crutches. Besides, what would he do at the dance?

Brendon's pal, Leo, wanted to fix Brendon up with Mandy, a girl Brendon liked in his English class. Leo kept pushing the idea; Brendon kept saying no. Without Brendon's consent, Leo told Mandy that Brendon wanted to ask her to the prom. Mandy said that she was already going with Steve. She told Brendon that he should ask for himself the next time. Brendon was bewildered. He didn't know that Leo had asked. He felt very angry at Leo for making this decision without okaying it with him first. Should he stifle his anger, knowing Leo meant well? Or should he be honest and tell Leo how he really felt? He did tell Leo. Leo couldn't understand how Brendon could be mad when Leo had only been trying to help.

- Are you afraid to assert yourself because you are afraid you'll lose friends? Do you feel uncomfortable expressing an opinion which differs from your friends'?

Start thinking about how and when you speak for yourself. It's important that you realize that you are unique, a one-of-a-kind person, an individual. Feel comfortable about the style in which you assert yourself. Some people speak very loudly and enthusiastically; people hear them clearly. Some people speak more softly and infrequently; they are heard equally clearly. Do not change your style. The key is to put into words exactly what you want or need.

Some general tips on being heard:

- Look the person you are talking to in the eye. If you are short or use a wheelchair, you will sometimes have to draw attention to yourself by speaking directly to the person. If he or she seems unwilling to look at you, you might find some clever—yet polite—way to say, "I'm right here." How you do that will depend on your personality. For someone who is extroverted, that might mean carrying a red bandana to wave. For someone who is more introverted, that might mean speaking in a louder, stronger voice.

- Speak clearly and distinctly in whatever way you can. If you have a speech disability, calm your anxiety by trying to relax the muscles in your body, taking in deep breaths of air and exhaling slowly. Speak slowly and as distinctly as you can. Sometimes it helps to calm yourself by visualizing a soothing image, such as a mountain stream or a quiet meadow in springtime. You will find that your whole body will relax and that you will be able to focus on your thoughts and your message. If you are calm, the other person will relax and be able to concentrate on what you are saying. If you use a speech synthesizer to speak, you may want to give the person a little note explaining this device. You will think of other ways to communicate.

- Be courteous and polite; say "please" and "thank you."

- Do not be overly polite (obsequious).

- If the person addresses everyone around you, but not you, tell the person nicely and firmly that you speak for yourself and that you would like to be addressed directly.
- Think about what you want to say and how you want to say it before you begin speaking.

Note: Assertiveness also means that you don't attack others in stating your needs. For instance, you don't berate the store clerk because the counters are too high for you to see over. That complaint will need to be given to the store owner/manager. Assertiveness means that you stand up for yourself in an adult, responsible way. It is not aggressive; it is not passive. Remember to keep the balance! And to be yourself!

▼ You're on Your Way

In this final section we've talked about many things you need to know about yourself to prepare for the future. Some of the issues we've looked at include:

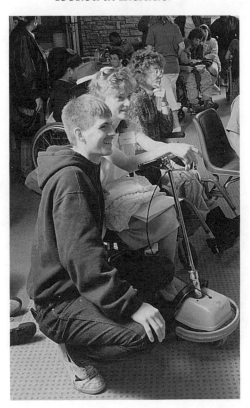

- What independence means to you and how to assess how independent you are.
- How you can begin to figure out your strengths and challenges.
- How disability affects your life.
- How and when to ask for help.
- How to let other know when you don't want any help.
- What expectations you have for yourself and what expectations others have for you—and how they sometimes clash.
- How and when to speak up for yourself.

Now is the time for you to begin your great adventure—life! To become an active, involved, interested, participating, caring person! To begin opening doors to the life you want to create for yourself . . . TO TAKE CHARGE!

AFTERTHOUGHTS

▼ ▼ ▼ ▼ ▼ ▼ ▼ ▼ ▼ ▼

If they were writing a chapter for this book, the teenagers interviewed for *Taking Charge* said they would make the following points:

Nicole: There *is* a pot of gold under a rainbow. You haven't found it yet. I would want my chapter to be like a conversation with a friend.

Tina: I would title it "Living Alone" and tell how it is being a disabled kid in school, shopping, cooking, living with a Canine Companion for Independence.

Glen: Entitled "A Handicapped Person's Guide to Life," my chapter would include my little hints or strategies for working around disability so your life doesn't revolve around disability.

Alyssa: Don't try to make people feel sorry for you. No one likes complaining. When someone first meets me, they see me as a sweet innocent. I'm not like that. Others never expect me to become involved with people who use drugs or alcohol. Although I don't use them, I'm faced with all the things ordinary people are. A lot of teens with disabilities have never faced things like keg parties. It blows their minds that I have.

Edward: I'd title it "Take It in Stride." I'd tell them to be yourself; try to be friendly. If you are a nice person, others will come to you. Do whatever you can physically.

June: Everyone is different in his own way. Be yourself. Get as much out of life as you can. Don't dwell on things you can't do. Have someone you can trust. Laugh at yourself. No one said life would be easy. Never put more weight on your shoulders than you can handle. Set high goals.

Myla: I'll tell them about disability; the problems and the things we deal with like other people. The title: "The Trouble with Disability."

Timeka: "One Person's Experience with a Physical Disability" would be the title. I would have teens be their own experts, as in *Taking Charge*.

Tim: The title would be "How to Survive." Get on with it. Don't worry. Look on the bright side; things could have been a lot worse. Hold your head up high. Don't look back.

WHAT YOU SHOULD KNOW ABOUT DISABILITY LAWS
*An Interview with David Capozzi**

▼　▼　▼　▼　▼　▼　▼　▼　▼　▼　▼

Ordinarily, you probably think of laws as rules telling you what you *can't* do: You can't drive through a red light, you can't help yourself to cookies in a grocery store without paying for them, you can't fudge your income on your federal tax return. But for young people with disabilities, some of the most important laws specify what you *can* do. In recent years, the federal government has passed a number of laws specifically aimed at benefiting people with disabilities. According to Mr. Capozzi, some of the most important are the IDEA, the ADA, the Rehabilitation Act of 1973, and the Air Carrier Access Act.

▼ The IDEA (Individuals with Disabilities Education Act)

This is a new name for an old law: The Education for All Handicapped Children Act of 1975 (Public Law 94–142). If you have ever received physical therapy, occupational therapy, speech-language therapy, or any other special educational service through your school, you have probably at least heard of this law. You may not be aware, however, of exactly what the IDEA means to you. Basically, it means that students with disabilities are entitled to receive a "free, appropriate education" in the "least restrictive environment." Furthermore, an "Individualized Education Program" (IEP) must be designed to meet each student's unique learning needs. Here's what these important provisions mean:

Free, Appropriate Education

▼ ▼

The "free" in this expression means exactly what it sounds like. Students with disabilities are entitled to receive a public school education at no cost to

---

*　David M. Capozzi is the Director of the Office of Technical and Information Services for the U.S. Architectural and Transportation Barriers Compliance Board. He has testified in support of the Americans with Disabilities Act (ADA) before the House Committee on Public Works and Transportation and was a member of the ADA "legal team" for the disability community that helped craft the legislative history and the final bill. As a member of a Federal Advisory Committee, he also helped negotiate regulations to implement the Air Carrier Access Act of 1986.

themselves or their parents. If there is no public school available that can serve their needs, then the public school system must pay for them to attend a private school. The "appropriate" in this expression is a little harder to understand. Two common misunderstandings are: 1) that it means that students with disabilities are entitled to receive the best possible education; or 2) that students with disabilities should receive an education that is as good as students without disabilities receive. Unfortunately, neither of these things is true. What "appropriate" really means is that you must receive an education that is reasonably certain to give you some benefit. Fortunately, students and their parents have some say in determining what kind of education is appropriate and will provide them some benefit. This is where the concepts of least restrictive environment and the individualized education program come in. (See below.)

Least Restrictive Environment

▼ ▼

This provision of the law requires that students with disabilities be mainstreamed as much as possible with nondisabled students. This means that if a student with a physical disability is capable of mastering the subjects taught in a regular classroom, he must be permitted to take his classes there. It also means that the school may have to make alterations to a classroom or provide special services to enable students with disabilities to be mainstreamed. For example, if a student with spina bifida wants to play trumpet in the band, but the band room is inaccessible to him because of the way the risers are placed, the school might have to build ramps. Or if someone who uses sign language to communicate is capable of learning calculus, but the only calculus teacher in the school can't understand sign language, the school would be required to find some way to allow the student to participate in class. The bottom line is that students with physical disabilities who have varying intellectual abilities cannot all be warehoused in the same classroom simply because other parts of the school building would require modification to be accessible.

Individualized Education Program

▼ ▼

You are probably familiar with the basic elements of an IEP. To review, they include:

1. a description of your present level of achievement;

2. short-term and long-term goals of your educational program;
3. the specific educational services you will receive;
4. the date services will start and how long they will last;
5. the methods (such as tests) that will be used to determine whether you are meeting your goals;
6. the extent to which you will be mainstreamed.

After you reach sixteen, your IEP must also include a plan for helping you make the transition to work or college after graduation. This is a fairly new requirement, so you may find yourself asking for specific kinds of transition help that your school does not yet routinely provide. Types of transition services your school may be required to provide, if appropriate, include: vocational training, training in independent living skills, and assistance in preparing for and making the transition to college. You, your parents, and school personnel should *jointly* decide what transition services you should receive, based on what you want to do after high school.

This brings up an important point: Transition planning is not the only way you can be involved in designing your IEP. Provided your parents consent, you can take part in every annual meeting held to discuss your education program. You can tell the school staff *in person* about any problems you are having in school and also suggest strategies for solving those problems. Sometimes the IEP meeting may appear to be an adversarial process, because schools are cutting back on funding. But if you can give a good argument about why you *need* a particular service—for example, a reader, a note taker, occupational therapy, or additional speech-language therapy—you just might get it.

What if you or your parents request a particular service, but you are turned down? If you can show that this means you are not receiving an appropriate education, you can fight the decision. The easiest way to resolve a dispute like this is for you and your parents to request a meeting with the IEP team, then try to work out a compromise. If the school staff won't budge, you can request a due process hearing. During a due process hearing, both you and the school are given the chance to present your side of the story before an impartial hearing officer. You can bring witnesses (doctors, teachers, therapists), show the hearing officer medical records, hire a lawyer to argue your case, or otherwise try to convince the hearing officer that you need the educational program you are requesting. After both you and the school have presented your side, the hearing officer will decide which side has the stronger case. To request a due process hearing, one of your parents can send a letter to your school district's Special Education Director, briefly explaining the nature of the dispute.

▼ The ADA (Americans with Disabilities Act)

After the IDEA, the Americans with Disabilities Act of 1990 is probably the single most important piece of disability legislation ever passed. Its purpose is to knock down virtually all remaining barriers that prevent people with disabilities from participating fully in their communities. There are provisions aimed at eliminating discrimination in employment, "public accommodations," telecommunications, and public transportation. Briefly, this is what these provisions cover:

Employment
▼ ▼ ▼ ▼ ▼ ▼ ▼ ▼ ▼ ▼

As of July 26, 1992, companies with 25 or more employees are prohibited from discriminating against qualified individuals with disabilities. As of July 26, 1994, companies with 15 or more employees may not discriminate. This means that if you are qualified to do a particular job, an employer cannot refuse to hire you, train you, or give you a promotion simply because you have a disability. Furthermore, employers are required to make "reasonable accommodation" to permit you to do the job properly, unless it would cause them "undue hardship." "Reasonable accommodation" means taking steps to remove barriers that make it difficult or impossible for you to do the job. Reasonable accommodation might include making the workplace more accessible to you, modifying office equipment so you can use it, changing some job responsibilities that require more physical strength or agility than you have, or providing an interpreter.

Public Accommodations
▼ ▼ ▼ ▼ ▼ ▼ ▼ ▼ ▼ ▼ ▼ ▼ ▼ ▼ ▼ ▼ ▼ ▼

This provision of the ADA prohibits discrimination by *any* business or facility that is open to the general public. Restaurants, hotels, theaters, parks, grocery stores, health clubs, hospitals, shopping centers, museums, bowling alleys—almost any business you can think of—must be open to individuals with disabilities under the same terms as they are open to individuals without disabilities. For example, a health club could not bar you from joining just because its locker room is not wheelchair accessible. (Instead, it might have to *make* the locker room accessible.) Or a restaurant could not refuse to let you use its dance floor because they think your wheelchair might get in the way of other dancers. Unless it would impose an un-reasonable cost, every business that is open to the public must allow people with disabilities to use their facilities on an equal footing with others.

Telecommunications

▼ ▼ ▼ ▼ ▼ ▼ ▼ ▼ ▼ ▼ ▼ ▼ ▼

By July 26, 1993, all telecommunications companies must make their services accessible to individuals with speech or hearing impairments. What this boils down to is that people who use a Telecommunications Device for the Deaf (TDD) must be able to communicate via telephone with people who do not have a TDD. The telecommunications companies will accomplish this via relay services. In addition, people with disabilities will not be charged any more to use telecommunications systems than people without disabilities.

Public Transportation

▼ ▼ ▼ ▼ ▼ ▼ ▼ ▼ ▼ ▼ ▼ ▼ ▼ ▼

This provision of the ADA is designed to ensure that all types of public transportation will be accessible to people with disabilities. As of August 26, 1990, public bus and rail systems cannot buy new vehicles unless they are accessible. (Unfortunately, public school buses can still segregate students with disabilities from able-bodied students. We expect people with disabilities to enter mainstream society as adults, yet we still separate them on school buses as children and young adults. It doesn't make much sense.)

Making the ADA Work for You

▼ ▼

The ADA is still relatively new, so it is difficult to tell how successful this law will be in creating a barrier-free society. In the meantime, what's the best way to use the ADA when you run up against a barrier? Mr. Capozzi suggests that you first make the manager or other person in charge aware of your problem in a non-threatening way. For example, if there are steps leading into a restaurant where a ramp could easily be installed, politely tell the manager that this is a problem for people in wheelchairs. Second, tell him or her about the ADA. Explain that it is good business practice to make his restaurant accessible, because you and your family would like to spend your money here. And by not having a ramp, his business is excluding 43 million people with disabilities who could potentially be customers. Tell the manager that it is the right thing to do. You could also let him know that there are tax incentives for businesses that make themselves more accessible. As of 1992, a business that removes barriers to comply with the ADA can take a tax deduction of up to $15,000 a year.

A number of agencies in the federal government can answer specific questions about the provisions of the ADA. See the Resources section for their addresses and phone numbers.

▼ The Rehabilitation Act of 1973

Before the ADA was passed, discrimination against individuals with disabilities was only outlawed in certain instances. For example, section 504 of the Rehabilitation Act of 1973 prohibited discrimination by federally funded programs only. This law is still in effect. It requires that any program or activity that receives federal funds make itself accessible so that people with disabilities can participate. Federally funded agencies include not only federal agencies, but also many job-training programs, schools and universities, transportation systems, recreation programs, and housing programs.

This law will become increasingly important to you as you graduate from high school and move on to college. For example, if a college class you are scheduled to take is on the second floor, but there is no elevator, the school must make the classroom accessible either by moving the class downstairs or by installing some type of lift.

▼ Air Carrier Access Act of 1986

This Act states in general that airlines may not discriminate against people with disabilities. In 1990, more specific regulations were created to give airlines and people with disabilities guidance. Now airlines cannot require a passenger with a disability to travel with an attendant. In addition, passengers with folding wheelchairs must be permitted to store them on board in the coat closet. If you do encounter a problem while traveling by plane, ask for the complaint resolution official with the airline for help resolving the problem. If you are still dissatisfied, you can file a formal complaint with the Department of Transportation. The address for Air Carrier Access Act complaints is: Consumer Affairs Department, U.S. Department of Transportation, 400 7th St., S.W., Washington, DC 20590.

▼ Advocating for Your Rights

Once you have a basic knowledge of the important laws that affect your life, you have the foundation to begin *advocating* (speaking up) for your rights. Although people with disabilities are often their own best advocates because they know themselves best, you don't have to go it alone. In high school, you can get help advocating from guidance counselors; local chapters of affiliates of disability groups such as Easter Seals; independent living centers; and government agencies. Sometimes law school students may be willing to act as a lay advocate to help you get the services you need. It's good experience for the law students, and a free service for people who need it. Once you reach college, the Office of Disabled Student Services will be a good place to turn for assistance. These offices are usually run *by* people with disabilities *for* people with disabilities. If all else fails, you always have the right to seek the advice of an attorney. Local chapters of disability organizations may be able to direct you to an attorney experienced in advocating for individuals with disabilities.

CAN YOU GET IN?
An Interview with Mark Mazz, AIA*

▼   ▼   ▼   ▼   ▼   ▼   ▼   ▼   ▼   ▼   ▼   ▼

Mark Mazz is an architect who specializes in barrier-free design and modification. In doing his work, Mr. Mazz keys in on the needs of the people who will use his designs.

Architects use two guidelines to help them in making a building accessible:

- building codes and standards; and
- reasonable accomodations.

Codes and standards contain specific regulations concerning accessibility. For instance, they might specify widths of doorways, heights of telephone booths, the degree of incline for ramps, and the design of bathrooms for use by persons in wheelchairs.

Codes generally are based on:

---

*   Mark Mazz is a registered Maryland architect specializing in barrier-free design and modification. He is with Celentano Esposito and Associates, Hyattsville, MD.

- American National Standards Institute (ANSI) guidelines (usually A117.1);
- the Uniform Federal Accessibility Standard (UFAS); or
- the Americans with Disabilities Act Accessibility Guidelines (ADAAG).

In addition to these national guidelines, there are state building codes, sometimes based on the ANSI guidelines. Some counties have their own codes which add requirements to state codes. Each state or county differs in the codes it adopts. In the future, the Americans with Disabilities Act Guidelines (ADAAG) will predominate.

Besides the codes and standards, something called "reasonable accommodations" should also be taken into account. Reasonable accommodations are modifications or adjustments needed to eliminate barriers so that a person with a disability has equal opportunity to use a building. In other words, the individual needs of the person with a disability should also be taken into account. Mr. Mazz sometimes pushes beyond the national and local codes to meet the needs of the individual user. For example, building codes might require that a bathroom be designed to be useable by someone in a wheelchair—that is, with plenty of room to maneuver the wheelchair and grab bars on the nearby walls to make it possible to swing in and out of the wheelchair. But if someone who uses crutches will be using the bathroom, he or she may need grab bars attached to the toilet itself. In designing an individual's home, the architect will be guided by the owner's specific needs. In public accommodations and reasonable accomodations, the codes will govern.

There are several ways you can find information about codes in your area. First, call the Information listing for your local county or city government. Tell the operator that you want the number for the Office for Persons with Disabilities or the Office for Handicapped Individuals. If there is no such listing, call the County Executive's or Mayor's office to ask which office deals with concerns of persons with disabilities. You can also find information through Independent Living Centers, which help persons with disabilities become more independent. To locate an Independent Living Center, contact your local hospital, rehabilitation center, or physical therapist. Your doctor should be able to help you as well. Finally, you can contact the Architectural and Transportation Barriers Compliance Board at 800–USA–ABLE for information on accessibility guidelines. If you want your own copy of the codes, expect to pay a fee. And, according to Mr. Mazz, "They are difficult to read!"

▼ Finding an Accessible Home

If you want to find an accessible place to live, where do you start? County agencies for persons with disabilities will often have lists of accessible apartments. Be aware, however, that these lists are often provided by owners who may think their apartments are accessible, but who may be ignorant of accessibility standards. A list does give you a starting place, though.

Call the apartment managers on the list before you visit. Types of questions you might ask include:

- Is there a stoop at the front door?
- Are there stairs to the front door?
- Is there a shower in the bathroom?
- Are there stairs in the apartment?
- How wide are corridors or hallways leading up to the apartment and within it?
- Any other question of major concern to you.

The answers to these questions should give you clues as to whether the apartment truly is accessible.

If you meet the income requirements, you may qualify for an apartment in a newer public housing project. By law, these projects must set aside a certain percentage of accessible units. Call your local public housing authorities for information on availability and eligibility guidelines.

If you are looking for a house, try to find a realtor in your area who is knowledgeable about accessibility. You can find one by calling individual reality agencies, or you can save yourself time and call your local government's Office for Persons with Disabilities. If you know someone with a disability who has rented or bought a home, ask him or her to refer you to knowledgeable realtors. You can also obtain housing information from local chapters of organizations that advocate for persons with disabilities, such as United Cerebral Palsy.

▼ Reporting Problems

What if you find violations of building codes? You need to report them to the codes enforcement arm of the government which has responsibility for the building. To find out what the codes enforcement arm is, contact the Building Permits Office. This office may be listed in the phone book under that title, or it may be housed in the Environmental Protection Office, the Environmental Resources Office, the Building Inspection and Permits Office, or the Environmental Management Office. Again, you can call your county or city information number to ask for the number of the Permits Office. Any architect or building contractor can also tell you how to find the Permits Office. A caution: Although a certain agency may be responsible for enforcing the codes, it may not have the funding to do so! If you aren't satisfied with the response you get from this agency, go to the local government Office for Persons with Disabilities. Let them either advocate for you or tell you what steps you should take next.

Many counties have 504 Compliance Committees, which check up on accessibility of government buildings. You can discover more about Section 504 of the Rehabilitation Act of 1973 in the interview with David Capozzi on page 129.

The federal agencies that can help you with accessibility problems are:

- Architectural and Transportation Barriers Compliance Board, and
- United States Department of Justice.

Information about contacting these agencies is given in the back of the book.

Mr. Mazz urges you to know your rights and to check on accessibility in your community. This is especially important to do in buildings that are built with our tax dollars. He encourages you to be someone who is willing to speak out when buildings are not accessible—to be a "squeaky wheel"!

TECHNOLOGICAL DEVELOPMENTS
An Interview with James Mueller*

▼   ▼   ▼   ▼   ▼   ▼   ▼   ▼   ▼   ▼

"... The success of accommodation is measured not in the achievements of technology, but in the achievements of people."
—from *The Workplace Workbook* by James Mueller

* James Mueller is an industrial designer and president of J.L. Mueller, Inc., in Chantilly, Virginia. He is especially interested in adapting environments for people with disabilities.

The quality of life for people with disabilities is constantly improving—thanks, in part, to an explosion of technological developments. Some noteworthy developments that industrial designer James Mueller singled out are described below. Remember, though, that technological changes are dynamic and rapid. The advances you read about here may already have been surpassed. To keep up-to-date on technological advances, you may want to contact some of the organizations listed at the end of the book. You can also refer to the listings of newsletters and directories for help locating current products.

▼ Personal Mobility

Wheelchair sports have done for wheelchairs what auto racing has done for cars. Wheelchairs, braces, and crutches are now lighter and smaller, as well as more maneuverable, durable, and cosmetically acceptable. Recent advances include: braces and protheses made of carbon-fiber instead of steel; wheelchairs powered by solid-state electronics instead of mechanical systems; faster-recharging batteries for wheelchairs; and collapsible or modular wheelchairs instead of rigid ones.

More improvements will come gradually. For instance, wheelchairs for special purposes, such as going to the beach or traveling over rough terrain, are constantly being developed and improved. And they are no longer made only of chrome and black vinyl. Competition is the key to developing more practical products. There used to be just one company producing wheelchairs in the U.S., for example. Now there are six or seven, plus foreign companies, working in the field. Costs of high-tech wheelchairs are still high but are likely to come down through competition.

▼ Vehicle Mobility

This is another area where giant strides are being made. It is getting easier for people with physical disabilities to travel via private vehicles *and* public transportation, thanks to competition and economic and legal pressures. Many people who wouldn't have been able to get around on their own twenty years ago are now able to.

More automobile manufacturers are now aware that people with disabilities buy cars, too. Some are offering modification packages that are more readily installed. And some include people with disabilities in their testing programs and consumer panels. The "big three" U.S. auto makers (Chrylser, Ford, and General Motors) are beginning to consider a variety of special needs and are working on alternative control systems. For example, they are testing a "joy-stick" (one-handed) control. And Volkswagen sells a van in which a lift can be installed and removed without modifying the van. Presently, many major auto manufacturers have programs offering advice about adaptations. They also offer purchasers of new cars a $500 rebate to offset the cost of installing control modifications.

Public transportation accessibility varies from city to city. But in most places, travel is becoming more reasonable and more dignified. Some of the many positive changes include wider aisles on airplanes, better-designed subway systems and trains, and increased use of para-transit vehicles of various types—usually accessible buses. Many of these changes are the direct result of the Americans with Disabilities Act (ADA). See "What You Should Know about Disability Laws" on page 129 for more on what the ADA has to say about transportation.

▼ Communication

Electronics research all over the world is leading to some exciting communications breakthroughs for people with speech difficulties. Some developments make it easier to use a computer to communicate. For example, Swedish scientists have developed armrests designed to glide over a keyboard for people who have little strength in their arms. There are also enlarged keyboards for people who can't use off-the-shelf models. Other developments enable people with little or no voice control to "speak" for the first time. Voice synthesizers with keyboard controls can be operated in scanning modes, or through blinking, nodding, or producing any consistent sound. These synthesizers can produce either male or female-sounding voices, adult or child. Prices for these devices remain high, but there are many more features for the money.

Progress is also being made in telecommunications. As you probably already know, "hands free" telephones (speaker-phones) are widely available. And it is now possible for TDD users to communicate (both send and receive) not only with other TDD users, but with users of regular phones. (TDD stands for Telecommunications Device for the Deaf, but it is also for people with speech difficulties.) This is done through a telephone company's relay system, which can receive messages either in written or voice form, then translate them to the opposite form. Also, telecommunications and computers can be integrated: a sound, a light sequence, head or eye movements, speech—almost any input—can be recognized and programmed to turn devices on or off, unlock doors, etc.

The Tele-Consumer Hotline is another telephone treasure. It is a non-profit, independent, impartial service that can suggest modifications or adaptations to make telephoning practical for people with limited mobility or hand use. You can reach them at: The Tele-Consumer Hotline, 1910 K St., N.W., Suite 610, Washington, DC 20006. Telephone: 800–332–1124 (Voice/TDD).

▼ Recreation

If enough people have the drive to show that they really want to participate in a sport or hobby, solutions may be developed. Most of the sports and hobbies that are now accessible to people with limited mobility are accessible only because of the efforts of enthusiasts. For example, technology now makes one-legged and wheelchair skiing possible, as well as sailing with limited mobility.

Unfortunately, few major companies place a high priority on helping people with disabilities take part in recreational activities. The Polaroid Company was an exception. It developed a program called "SNAP" (Special Needs Adapted Photography) aimed at making photography more accessible. Although the SNAP program is no longer active, you can still find cameras that are designed to be operated with one hand, that have remote shutter buttons, or that have self-timers with built-in delay.

If the adaptation you need is not commercially available, this may be a good time to turn to a handyman for help devising a solution. A local chapter of the Volunteers for Medical Engineering might also be able to help. (See "To Make It Happen.")

(Also remember that not all sports and hobby adaptations need be high-tech. As Cynthia Lins, Physical Education Specialist with the Montgomery County (MD) Public Schools suggests, you can ask a physical or occupational therapist for help adapting equipment or locating resources. Velcro applied to balls and paddles can be very helpful. Therapeutic horseback riding and beep-ball leagues are available in many communities. Special Olympics at local levels are often open to everyone who has disabilities, even though they are only for people with mental disabilities at state and national levels. Local wheelchair associations may sponsor wheelchair sports events, as may the national wheelchair organizations listed at the back of the book. Finally, your city or county recreation department will be able to guide you to activities that are both feasible and fun.)

▼ Employment

Opportunity is the big issue. Today's workers with disabilities have greater opportunities to show what they can do because of the Americans with Disabilities Act and the increasing sensitivity of employers. Technological advancements are also making it easier to fit into the workplace. "White collar" jobs, for example, are becoming less physically and mentally demanding. Computers can make it possible to deliver work electronically, rather than by hand. Spelling and grammar can be checked through computer programs. Office doorways and work stations can be modified to accommodate wheelchairs; files can be made accessible; remote controls can switch equipment on and off; communication can be made possible through a variety of spoken and written systems.

In addition, there are now federally funded vocational rehabilitation centers around the country. As the sidebar on page 143 explains, these rehabilitation centers can help you obtain or learn how to use adaptive equipment needed for a job. Along with private organizations and associations, they make employment for people with disabilities a rapidly expanding field. The climate is encouraging, and there is almost no limit except one's own ambition.

TO MAKE IT HAPPEN
*An Interview with John H. Staehlin**

▼ ▼ ▼ ▼ ▼ ▼ ▼ ▼ ▼ ▼ ▼ ▼

"The needs are there, the technology exists—the challenge is to make it happen!"

—VME, Inc.

Computers and other technological developments have given many people with disabilities new options for relationships, employment, and recreation. A piece of equipment might be very helpful to you, but how do you reach it, how do you switch it on and off, and how do you control it?

Volunteers for Medical Engineering (VME), Inc. is one group that is actively searching for ways to help people with specific limitations of move-

---

*   John H. Staehlin is a consulting engineer for Westinghouse. He is the founder and president of Volunteers for Medical Engineering (VME), Inc., 5202 Westland Blvd., Baltimore, MD 21227.

Paying for Equipment

What good is the new technology if you can't afford it? Unfortunately, most types of health insurance do not cover costs of equipment such as wheelchairs and computers. In the future, this situation may improve, if enough individuals and groups bring lawsuits challenging the denial of insurance claims. For now, there are several other avenues that you can take to request financial assistance for needed equipment:

• If your insurance company denies a claim, you can try to challenge that denial by applying to the company headquarters or home office, but there is no guarantee that they will reverse the decision.

• Your state Vocational Rehabilitation Office may have limited funds to help purchase items *if* they are work-related. The office might also train you to use the equipment at no cost.

• Most states have federally funded Technology Assistance Programs (T.A.P.) that can help identify possible sources of private funding for adaptive equipment. These programs are mandated by Public Law 100–407, Title I, 1988. Sources for funding might include Medicare/Medicaid, school systems, and civic or service organizations. You can get the address and phone number of your state's T.A.P. through RESNA, Suite 700, 1101 Connecticut Ave. N.W., Washington, DC 20036; telephone: 202–857–1140.

• You may also be able to get financial assistance for communication or mobility devices through the Early Periodic Screening, Diagnosis and Treatment Program, a Medicaid waiver program. Contact your local Social Security Office for information about EPSDT.

For more information on sources of financial assistance, write to request these free publications: "Assistive Technology: Becoming an Informed Consumer," available from NICHCY, P.O. Box 1492, Washington, DC 20013; and *NARIC QUARTERLY* (Winter 1989 issue), available from NARIC, 8455 Colesville Rd., Suite 935, Silver Spring, MD 20910.

ment or control. Since 1982, the non-profit organization has been adapting commercially available equipment and creating new equipment. The first chapter of VME was started in Baltimore, Maryland. Today there are about fifteen chapters across the country, and more are forming. (See below.)

The volunteers who donate their time to VME are from companies such as Westinghouse, General Dynamics, Martin Marietta, Polaroid, DuPont, McDonnell Douglas, and Exxon. Many smaller companies also get involved with specific projects. And university engineering students often help out and get valuable hands-on experiences. Mr. Staehlin writes: "Our charter is to mobilize the brainpower in aerospace and defense corporations and apply that ingenuity to the solution of problems of disability and aging."*

Examples of VME innovations include:

- a hand-closure device that enables a quadraplegic man to grasp objects
- a "blinkswitch" that allows users to use eye-blinks to operate computer-driven communication boards and environmental controls such as light and sound systems
- a curved keyboard that makes all computer keys accessible to a man who uses a mouth-stick
- a hand-driven "standing wheelchair" called the Mobile Standing Frame, which is going to be mass-produced
- a big-key calculator with keys spaced about a half-inch apart, permitting a girl who has cerebral palsy to take trigonometry at school.

A huge new undertaking of VME is "Future Home." Future Home is a demonstration house in Maryland that is being remodeled as a living laboratory for a man with quadriplegia and his wife. This "intelligent" house will show how people with disabilities can perform everyday tasks using automation technology. It will demonstrate that any consistent signal—including disabled speech—can control doors, lights, TV, kitchen and laundry appliances, etc. Future Home will provide solid evidence that independent living is feasible for many people with physical disabilities.

VME has also started a loan program so that equipment designed for someone who no longer needs it can be used by someone else. This program, called DCAT (Distribution Center for Assistive Technology), charges reasonable fees for services. Other VME programs are underway, and more are planned.

---

* *Leaders,* vol. 14, no. 1 (Jan.-March, 1991), 50.

If there is a VME chapter in your area, feel free to contact them and ask for help with a specific problem. Solutions may take time and patience, but they will be pursued. Currently, there are VME chapters in: Auburn and Harvest, AL; Wilmingon, DE; Tampa, FL; Idaho Falls, ID; Boston, MA; Baltimore, MD; St. Louis, MO; Pittsburgh, PA; Oakridge, TN: College State, Dallas, and Fort Worth, TX; Charlottsville and Newport News, VA; and Seattle, WA. If you cannot locate the VME office in your area, phone the national headquarters at 410–455–6395.

If there is no VME chapter in your area, you may still be able to find someone who can help adapt or construct equipment to expand your opportunities for mobility, communication, employment, or recreation. Try asking a physical therapist, occupational therapist, or speech-language pathologist to suggest an interested engineer, technician, or handyman—or woman.

HOW DO YOU TAKE CHARGE OF YOUR BODY?
An Interview with Arthur Siebens, M.D.*

▼ ▼ ▼ ▼ ▼ ▼ ▼ ▼ ▼ ▼ ▼ ▼ ▼

Taking charge of your life includes learning about your body and starting to make decisions about what is good for you now and in the future. You need to learn how and where to get information about your physical needs, and how to talk with health professionals.

Dr. Arthur Siebens stresses the need for you to become an expert on yourself and your needs. He says, "Any question is legitimate," so don't be embarrassed to ask anything you want to know. Sometimes your doctor may not have the answer, either because he or she doesn't have the knowledge, or because the answer is unknown. But that doesn't mean you shouldn't ask your question.

Dr. Siebens suggests that you consider the following questions:

1. What can I expect of my body now and with the passage of time?

Only a doctor experienced in treating people with your disability can answer this question. Finding a doctor who is willing and able to tell you

---

* Dr. Arthur Siebens is Professor of Rehabilitation Medicine at the Johns Hopkins School of Medicine in Baltimore. He is also the director of the Department of Rehabilitation Medicine at Good Samaritan Hospital in Baltimore.

what to expect may be difficult, but it is worth the search. You must become realistic about what you can expect to deal with in the future. Reality is easier to deal with than uncertainty.

2. How can I make a wise choice in selecting a doctor?

Here are some suggestions for gathering information about doctors in your area:

- Find out whether your local hospital has a referral service that can provide information about specialists, their backgrounds, office locations, and fee schedules.
- Ask someone in a hospital for children with disabilities or the hospital department of rehabilitation to recommend an appropriate physician.
- Contact the national organization for your disability and ask them to recommend a specialist in your disability.
- If you have been seeing a pediatrician, ask him or her to recommend someone you can see when you're older—perhaps a rehabilitation physician or a physician with expertise in treating people with your disability.

3. How should I prepare for my doctor's appointment?

- When you make an appointment, be sure to schedule enough time. If it is your first visit with this physician, prepare a summary of your condition and of important treatments such as surgical events, current medications, and their results. It helps if you obtain medical summaries of previous hospitalizations or office medical care by writing to the hospital medical records department and/or your physicians.
- Think about all of your concerns ahead of time. Then write down your questions. Make good use of your time.
- If you have or use braces, orthotics, or prostheses, bring them with you to the appointment.
- Find out what you can expect from the physician (such as 24–hour-a-day coverage) and what your responsibilities are in the relationship (being on time for appointments, having questions ready).
- If you get along, continue the relationship. If you feel that the first meeting has not been adequate, make another appoint-

ment. Ask the physician if he or she would welcome a continuing relationship.

- Over the long term, try to develop a vocabulary of medical terms about your disability by reading books and magazines and by talking to medical professionals in different fields. This will enable you to accurately describe what you want to know. You will also be better able to understand what the doctor is saying.

4. Once I've established a relationship, how do I work with my health care professionals to get the most out of my medical rehabilitation plan?

Whether you are a teenager or an adult, you need to take responsibility for becoming part of the rehabilitation team. Health care professionals will be more likely to treat you as part of the team if you are straightforward and thoughtful when you talk with them. Remember, professionals have feelings, too, and react personally to the people they are working with. They will be most interested in helping you if you are considerate and have a positive attitude.

You will react emotionally to certain procedures, decisions, and interactions with people in the medical profession. Some professionals will understand how you feel and respond to your emotions. Some will not be able to do so. This does not make your feelings wrong. You just need to understand that the person you are dealing with does not understand. You may always change your doctor or therapist if you don't think he or she is responsive to your feelings or if you are not satisfied with the service provided. Making this decision is one of your responsibilities.

5. How can I gain some control over decision making about my own medical care plan?

Your best bet is to be well informed about yourself. Then try to identify goals that meet your needs and appear within your reach. This will require time: time to become informed, time to adjust to the information, time to speak with people, time to formulate questions. In setting goals and seeking information, think about all aspects of your life, including activities of daily living, your health, your educational and vocational plans, and your sexuality.

6. What are some special physical considerations for persons with disabilities to keep in mind?

Diet and exercise are important considerations. Since a physical disability limits energy output and the capacity for exercise, you need to watch the amount of food you eat. Otherwise, you are more likely to gain weight. To find out what the right diet is for you, you might want to consult a dietician. Your doctor will be able to refer you to one. Your school may also have a dietician.

To ensure you get proper exercise, ask your doctor to recommend a physical therapist. The physical therapist can tailor a program of home exercise to meet your individual needs. You could also call health clubs to see if they have programs for people with disabilities. If you have college plans, look into special physical education programs for students with disabilities.

7. Besides talking to my personal physician, how can I get the information and help I need to deal with my medical concerns?

You are not alone. You can find the help you need if you search. Dr. Siebens recommends these resources:

- your pediatrician or family doctor
- rehabilitation nurses
- your school or public library (ask the librarian for books on health, how the body works, medical diagnoses)
- rehabilitation physicians
- speech and language pathologists
- physical and occupational therapists
- social workers
- psychologists
- books in the health, science, or medical sections of bookstores and libraries
- periodicals and newspapers
- organizations such as United Cerebral Palsy and Spina Bifida Association of America
- state and national governmental offices for persons with disabilities
- computer data banks, such as Project Word on page 158
- "hot line" telephone services for information on AIDS or other medical concerns

You will probably be able to think of other resources in your own community.

8. How do I deal with my feelings about what goes on physically with my body?

You may want to find someone outside your family or friends to talk with about your disability and its impact on your life. Some resources include:

- psychologists
- social workers
- rehabilitation counselors
- psychiatrists
- ministers, rabbis, or priests
- school counselors
- peer organizations (support groups, church groups, etc.)

Books by people who have learned to deal with disability and to enjoy life are helpful, as are magazines such as those listed on page 156.

Dr. Siebens emphasizes that you are not alone. Others have the same challenges as you. Networking with them and with professionals will increase your understanding of your disability as well as your ability to cope.

RESOURCES

Listed below are a few of the many books, magazines, organizations, and other resources that can help you gather information on specific subjects and become involved. There is not enough space to print all that is available. Use these suggestions to begin your own personal search.

▼ Directories of Products and Services

Abrams, A. Jay and Margaret Ann Abrams. *The First Whole Rehab Catalog: A Comprehensive Guide to Products and Services for the Physically Disadvantaged*. Betterway Publications (Box 219, Crozet, VA), 1990. 240 pages with photos. $16.95. Includes sections on home management, personal care, accessibility, communication, mobility, transportation, health and fitness, recreation, and education and vocation, plus listings of catalogs, books, and organizations.

Berliss, Jane R., Peter A. Borden, Kelly Ford, and Gregg Vanderheiden, editors. *Trace Resource Book: Assistive Technologies for Communication, Control and Computer Access*. Trace Research and Development Center (S–151 Waisman Center, 1500 Highland Ave., Madison, WI 53705), 1991–92. 887 pages with photos and drawings. $50.00. Has sections on communication aids, switches and environmental controls, computer adaptations, application software for special education, and rehabilitation. Appendices list additional product information, information resources, service providers, and organizations.

Enders, Alexandra and Marian Hall, editors. *Assistive Technology Source Book*. RESNA Press (Suite 700, 1101 Connecticut Ave., Washington, DC 20036), 1990. 576 pages. Includes information on search strategies; information resources; assessment; equipment evaluation; follow-through; safety; personal and home care; education; employment; recreation/leisure technology; mobility; communication; control; computer access; medical treatment issues; audio-visual resources.

Shrout, Richard Neal. *Resource Directory for the Disabled: A Guide for the Hearing, Vision, and Mobility Impaired*. Facts on File (460 Park Ave. South, New York, NY 10016), 1991. 391 pages. $45.00. Includes general sections on travel, recreation, and social opportunities; organizations, associations, and support groups; employment and training opportunities and education. Sections specifically for people with mobility impairments include: appliances, devices, and other aids; using computers; travel help; recreation, sports, and social opportunities; employment and training; and publications of interest.

▼ Sexuality and Genetics

Ayrault, Evelyn West. *Sex, Love, and the Physically Handicapped*. The Continuum Publishing Company (575 Lexington Avenue, New York, NY 10022), 1981. (Out of print, but may still be available in libraries.)

Bloom, Beth-Ann and Edward Seljeskog, M.D. *A Parent's Guide to Spina Bifida.* University of Minnesota Press (2073 University Avenue, S.E., Minneapolis, MN 55414), 1988.

Dechesne, B.H., C. Pons, and A. Schellen, eds. *Sexuality and Handicap: Problems of Motor-Handicapped People.* Charles C. Thomas (2600 South First Street, Springfield, IL 62794), 1986. (Out of print, but may still be available in libraries.)

Duffy, Yvonne. *...all things are possible.* A.J. Garvin & Associates (P.O. Box 7525, Ann Arbor, MI 48107), 1981.

Ferreyra, Susan and Katrine Huges. *Table Manners: A Guide to the Pelvic Examination for Disabled Women and Health Care Providers.* Sex Education for Disabled People, Planned Parenthood Alameda/San Francisco (1660 Bush Street, San Francisco, CA 94109), 1982.

"Healthy Adolescent Sexual Development," Part II. SIECUS Report, Vol. 18, No. 1, Oct.-Nov. 1989. Sex Information and Education Council of the U.S. (32 Washington Place, New York, NY 10003).

Kroll, Ken and Erica Levy Klein. *Enabling Romance: A Guide to Love, Sex, and Relationships for the Disabled (and the people who care about them).* Harmony Books/New York, a division of Crown Publishers (201 E. 50th Street, New York, NY 10022), 1992.

National Genetics Foundation (NGF), 555 W. 57th St., New York, NY 10019. For a small charge, NGF will do a computerized analysis of an individual's family health history to identify health problems that may be passed on to the individual's children. The completed analysis is sent to the individual's physician.

Pierce, Benjamin A. *The Family Genetic Sourcebook.* John Wiley and Sons, Inc. (Professional & Trade Division, 605 Third Avenue, New York, NY 10158), 1990.

Planned Parenthood Federation of America, 2010 Massachusetts Ave., N.W., Washington, DC 20036. Telephone: 202–785–3351.

Sex Information and Education Council of the U.S. (SEICUS), 130 W. 42nd St., Suite 2500, New York, NY 10036. Telephone: 212–819–9770.

Task Force on Concerns of Physically Disabled Women, Susan Shaul, ed. *Toward Intimacy—Family Planning and Sexuality Concerns of Physically Disabled Women.* Human Sciences Press/Plenum Publishing Corporation (233 Spring St., New York, NY 10013), 1978.

▼ Back to Nature/Travel

Courage Center, 3915 Golden Valley Rd., Golden Valley, MN 55422. Telephone: 612–588–0811. Operates Camp Courage, a residential camp program for ages 8 and older.

Roth, Wendy and Michael Tompane. *Easy Access to National Parks.* Sierra Club Books (100 Bush St., San Francisco, CA 94104). A guide to places in national parklands that are accessible to travelers with physical disabilities, including those with vision and hearing impairments.

Travel Information Service, Moss Rehabiliation Hospital, 1200 W. Tabor Rd., Philadelphia, PA 19141. Telephone: 215–456–9600. For a small fee, will prepare an information packet on accessible travel to a specific destination.

Wilderness Inquiry, Inc., 1313 5th St. S.E., Box 84, Minneapolis, MN 55414–1546. Phone: 800–728–0719. Wilderness (land and water) excursions combining persons with and without disabilities.

Wilderness on Wheels Foundation, 7125 W. Jefferson Ave., No. 155, Lakewood, CO 80235. Accessible camping, hiking, and fishing for people with disabilities.

▼ Communication and Technology

Accent on Information (AOI), P.O. Box 700, Bloomington, IN 61702. Telephone: 309–378–2961. Operates a database of information on products that assist people with disabilities and on activities of daily living. For a small fee, AOI will perform a search on any topic and give you the information available on that topic.

American Speech-Language-Hearing Association (ASHA), 10801 Rockville Pike, Rockville, MD 20852. Telephone: 301–897–5700. Can recommend speech-language pathologists in your area, as well as hearing specialists and augmentative communication specialists.

AT&T National Special Needs Center, 2001 Rte. 46, Suite 310, Parsippany, NJ 07054. Telephone: 800–233–1222 or 800–833–3232 (TDD). Staff can suggest solutions to telecommunications problems of people with disabilities.

IBM National Support Center for Persons with Disabilities, P.O. Box 2150, Atlanta, GA 30301. Telephone: 800–426–2133 or 800–284–9482 (TDD). Offers information on how computers can benefit people with disabilities in school, at work, and at home. Can describe technology that is available and provide a list of suppliers of equipment.

International Society for Augmentative and Alternative Communication (ISAAC), P.O. Box 1762, Station R, Toronto, Ontario, Canada M4G 4A3.

RESNA, Suite 700, 1101 Connecticut Ave., Washington, DC 20036. Publishes a free newsletter, *A.T. Quarterly*, which provides updates on assistive technology. Also publishes *Assistive Technology and the I.E.P.*, available for $10.

The Tele-Consumer Hotline, 1910 K St., N.W., Suite 610, Washington, DC 20006. Telephone: 800–332–1124 (Voice/TDD). Can suggest ways to modify or adapt equipment to make telephoning easier for people with limited mobility or hand use.

Trace Research and Development Center on Communication, Control and Computer Access for Handicapped Individuals, S–151 Waisman Center, 1500 Highland Ave., Madison, WI 53705. Telephone: 608–262–6966 or 608–263–5408 (TDD). Can refer individuals with disabilities to sources of information about augmentative communication, software, related professionals. For a small charge, offers booklets on augmentative communication systems and computers.

Volunteers for Medical Engineering, 5202 Westland Blvd., Baltimore, MD 21227. See page 142 for description.

▼ Education

HEATH Resource Center, One Dupont Circle, N.W., Suite 800, Washington, DC 20036–1193. Telephone: 800–544–3284 or 202–939–9320. HEATH (Higher Education and Adult Training for people with Handicaps) is a clearinghouse on postsecondary education for individuals with disabilities that is funded by the U.S. Dept. of Education. It offers a variety of free publications, including "Financial Aid for Students with Disabilities," "Vocational Rehabilitation Services—A Student Consumer's Guide," "$$$ for Adaptive Technology," and "How to Choose a College: Guide for the Student with a Disability." Request a publications list for a list of other titles available.

Pope, Loren. *Looking Beyond the Ivy League: Finding the College That's Right for You.* Viking Penguin (375 Hudson St., New York, NY 10014), 1990. 288 pages. $10.95.

Thomas, James L. and Carol H. Thomas. *Directory of College Facilities & Services for People with Disabilities.* 3rd ed. Oryx Press (4041 N. Central at Indian School Rd., Phoenix, AZ 85012), 1991. $115. This one has a hefty price tag, so look for it in your library.

Tweed, Prudence K. and Jason C. Tweed. *Colleges That Enable: A Guide to Support Services Offered to Physically Disabled Students on 40 U.S. Campuses.* Park Avenue Press, 1989. 106 pages. $10.95.

▼ Legal Questions and Problems

For Questions about the Americans with Disabilities Act (ADA)

ADA HOTLINE: 800–4664–ADA

EMPLOYMENT questions:

Equal Employment Opportunity Commission
  Review and Appeals Division
  1801 L St., N.W.
  Washington, DC 20507
  Telephone: 800–669–EEOC (voice); 800–800–3302 (TDD)

TRANSPORTATION questions:

U.S. Dept. of Transportation

Office of the Assistant General Counsel for
    Regulation and Enforcement
  400 7th St., S.W.

Washington, DC 20590
Telephone: 202–366–9305; 202–755–7687 (TDD)

ARCHITECTURAL ACCESSIBILITY questions:

Architectural and Transportation Barriers Compliance Board
1111 18th St., N.W., Suite 501
Washington, DC 20036
Telephone: 800–USA–ABLE (voice and TDD)

PUBLIC ACCOMMODATION questions:

U.S. Department of Justice
Office of Americans with Disabilities Act
P.O. Box 66118
Washington, DC 20035–6118
Telephone: 202–514–0301 (voice); 202–514–0383

TELECOMMUNICATIONS questions:

Federal Communication Commission
Consumer Assistance
1919 M St., N.W.
Washington, DC 20554
Telephone: 202–632–7260 (voice); 202–632–6999 (TDD)

Other Legal Resources

Consumer Affairs Dept., U.S. Dept. of Transportation, 400 7th St., S.W., Washington, DC 20590. Address for registering Air Carrier Access Act complaints.

Disability Rights Education and Defense Fund (DREDF), 2212 6th St., Berkeley, CA 94710. Telephone: 415–644–2555. A nonprofit organization dedicated to furthering the civil rights of people with disabilities. Can provide information on disability rights laws and policies. Publishes *Disability Rights News* three times a year, available free.

Index of Resource Materials on Fair Housing for People with Disabilities. Available for $1.00 from Community Watch MHLP, 1101 15th St., N.W., Suite 1212, Washington, DC 20005.

Office for Civil Rights, U.S. Dept. of Education, 400 Maryland Ave., S.W., Washington, DC 20202. Telephone: 202–205–5413. Investigates charges of discrimination brought against programs and activities (including schools) that receive federal funds from the Dept. of Education. Also offers a free pamphlet about Section 504 of the Rehabilitation Act of 1973.

▼ Support Dogs

Canine Companions for Independence (CCI), 1215 Sebastopol Rd., Santa Rosa, CA 95407. Telephone: 707–528–0830.

Phydeaux's for Freedom, Inc., 1 Main St., Laurel, MD 20707. Telephone: 410–880–4178. A support dog training facility.

▼ Magazines

Check your library for these magazines, or write for subscription information.

Accent on Living. Cheever Publishing, Inc., Gillum Rd. and High Dr., P.O. Box 700, Bloomington, IL 61702. Published quarterly. Includes information on products and techniques for people with disabilities; true life stories.

Disability Rag. Avocado Press, Inc., Box 145, Louisville, KY 40201. Six issues per year.

Horizons, News by and for People with Disabilities. P.O. Box 985, Gambrills, MD 21054. Published monthly.

Mainstream, Magazine of the Able-Disabled. 2973 Beech St., San Diego, CA 92102. Published monthly, except in January and June.

Spinal Network Extra. P.O. Box 4162, Boulder, CO 80306. Telephone: 303–449–5412. Quarterly magazine for people who use wheelchairs.

For additional information on periodicals:

NARIC Guide to Disability and Rehabilitation Periodicals, Providing Information for an Independent Life. Silver Spring, MD: NARIC, 1991. Titles, addresses, subscription information about periodicals on the following topics: administration, advocacy, counseling, health care, independent living, special education, specific disabilities, technology, vocational training and employment. Order from NARIC, 8455 Colesville Rd., Silver Spring, MD 20910.

▼ Disability Organizations and Special Events

Adolescent Employment Readiness Center, Room 1336, 111 Michigan Ave., N.W., Washington, DC 20010–2970. A project designed to help teenagers with disabilities develop pre-employment readiness skills that will lead to future employment.

American Chronic Pain Association, P.O. Box 850, Rocklin, CA 95677. Telephone: 916–632–0922. A nonprofit organization with over 400 chapters in the U.S., Canada, Australia, and New Zealand. Provides a support system for individuals with chronic pain through group activities, and offers training in skills and attitudes helpful in dealing with chronic pain.

Clearinghouse on Disability Information, Office of Special Education and Rehabilitative Services, U.S. Dept. of Education, Room 3132, Switzer Building, Washington, DC 20202. Telephone: 202–205–8241. Can provide information on federal programs benefiting people with disabilities and on federal disability legislation. *Pocket Guide to Federal Help for Individuals with Disabilities,* a summary of benefits and services available to qualified individuals, is available free of charge.

Coalition of Heritable Disorders of Connective Tissue, 382 Main St., Port Washington, NY 11050. Telephone: 516–883–8712. Promotes research about genetic connective tissue disorders.

HOW (Handicapped's Only a Word) Conference. Annual conference for teenagers with physical disabilities, their parents, and their teenaged siblings. Held in Montgomery County, MD. For more information, call or write: Kay Harris Kriegsman or Kendra Wells, co-directors, at the Montgomery County Cooperative Extension Service, 18410 Muncaster Mill Rd., Derwood, MD 20855. Telephone: 301–590–9638.

March of Dimes Birth Defects Foundation, 1275 Mamaroneck Ave., White Plains, NY 10605. Telephone: 914–428–7100. The March of Dimes strives to prevent birth defects through research, education, advocacy, and community services. They offer free fact sheets on many genetic disorders.

Muscular Dystrophy Association, 3561 East Sunrise Dr., Tucson, AZ 85718. Telephone: 602–529–2000.

National Ataxia Foundation, 600 Twelve Oaks Center, 15500 Wayzata Blvd., Wayzata, MN 55391. Telephone: 612–473–7666.

National Center for Youth with Disability (NCYD), Box 721—UMHC, Harvard St. at East River Rd., Minneapolis, MN 55455. Telephone: 800–333–6293 or 612–626–2825. An information and resource center focusing on adolescents with chronic illnesses or disabilities and the issues associated with making the transition to adult life. Staff can answer questions about training, education, and other transition issues; make referrals to other resources; and search the NCYD data base.

National Easter Seal Society, 70 East Lake St., Chicago, IL 60601. Telephone: 312–726–6200. A nonprofit organization dedicated to increasing the independence of people with disabilities through research and services. Local affiliates offer therapies, counseling, and vocational assistance, and advocate on behalf of people with disabilities.

National Information Center for Children and Youth with Disabilities (NICHCY), P.O. Box 1492, Washington, DC 20013. Telephone: 800–999–5599 or 703–893–6061. A federally funded project that collects and shares information helpful to children and adolescents with disabilities and the people who care about them. Staff members can answer questions about options and services for people with disabilities. Also offers free publications on many disability-related issues. Request a publications list.

National Organization on Disability, 910 16th St., N.W., Washington, DC 20006. Telephone: 800–248–ABLE or 202–293–5960. A privately funded organization that works to integrate people with disabilities into their communities.

Osteogenesis Imperfecta Foundation, P.O. Box 14807, Clearwater, FL 34629. Telephone: 813–855–7077.

President's Committee on Employment of People with Disabilities, 1111 20th St., N.W., Washington, DC 20036. Telephone: 202–653–5044. Advocates for and increases public awareness of job opportunities for people with disabilities. Offers pamphlets, a monthly newsletter (*Tips and Trends*), and a quarterly magazine (*Worklife*). Sponsors the Job Accommodation Network, a data base that provides information to help solve accomodation problems for workers with disabilities. All services are free.

Project WORD, Inc., 4085 University Dr., Suite 307, Fairfax, VA 22030. Telephone: 703–273–6789. Information and referral service on activities of daily living, and vocational, recreational, and medical information.

Spina Bifida Association of America, 1700 Rockville Pike, Suite 250, Rockville, MD 20852. Telephone: 800–621–3141 or 301–770–7222.

Spinal Cord Society, Wendell Rd., Fergus Falls, MN 56537. Telephone: 218–739–5252. For people with spinal cord injuries and their families, as well as scientists and physicians.

United Cerebral Palsy Associations, 7 Penn Plaza, Suite 804, New York, NY 10001. Telephone: 800–USA–1UCP or 212–268–6655.

For additional information about organizations:

Directory of National Information Sources on Disabilities. The National Insitute on Disability and Rehabilitation Research, Office of Special Education and Rehabilitation Services, 400 Maryland Ave., S.W., Washington, DC 20202, Attn.: Research Information Officer. Telephone: 202–205–8134. This 555–page book published in 1991 lists organizations supplying disability-related information, referral, and other services on a nationwide basis. Free while supplies last. (Also available for $5 from: NARIC, 8455 Colesville Rd., Silver Spring, MD 20910.)

▼ Wheelchair/Disabled Sports Programs

National Handicapped Sports and Recreation Association, 1145 19th St., N.W., Suite 717, Washington, DC 20036. Telephone: 301–652–7505.

National Handicapped Winter Sports, c/o National Handicapped Sports and Recreation Association, 1145 19th St., N.W., Suite 717, Washington, DC 20036. Telephone: 301–652–7505.

National Wheelchair Athletic Association, 3595 E. Fountain Blvd., Suite L1, Colorado Springs, CO 80910. Telephone: 719–574–1150.

Sports and Spokes—The Magazine for Wheelchair Sports and Recreation, 5201 N. 19th Ave., Suite 111, Phoenix, AZ 85015.

▼ Youth Organizations

The groups listed below welcome all young people, with or without disabilities. Look for listings of locations in your local phone directory.

  4–H Clubs
  Boy Scouts of America
  Girl Scouts of America
  YWCA
  YMCA
  Youth groups of religious denominations

▼ For Brothers and Sisters

Sibling Information Network, A.J. Pappanikou Center, University Affiliated Program, 991 Main St., E. Hartford, CT 06108. Telephone: 203–282–7050. Members receive a quarterly newsletter about issues related to siblings of children with disabilities and their problems. Can provide a list of sibling groups and programs.

INDEX

Abilities, identifying, 93–95

Accessibility, building, 17, 71, 73, 122, 134, 135–40

ADA, 72, 132–34

Adaptive equipment, 108, 139–45, 151. *See also* Communication devices

Advocacy, 135. *See also* Assertiveness

Aggressiveness, 117

AIDS, 31

Air Carrier Access Act of 1986, 134

Airplanes, 134, 140

Americans with Disabilities Act. *See* ADA

Anger. *See* Emotions

Apartments, accessible, 137

Apathy, 22

Appearance. *See also* Self-image
concerns about, 31–33, 40–41
indifference to own, 22

Architectural and Transportation Barriers Compliance Board, 136

Arthritis, 28

Assertiveness, 117–25. *See also* Advocacy
definition of, 117
others' reactions to, 119–20
reasons for, 120–23
tips on, 124–25

Assistance. *See* Help

Assistive technology. *See* Adaptive equipment

Ataxia, 157

Augmentative communication. *See* Communication devices

Automobiles, 139–40

Bathrooms, non-accessible, 73

Birth control, 30. *See also* Sexuality

Boyfriends. *See* Dating; Friends

Braces, 139

Brothers and sisters
embarrassment about, 58–60
resentment between, 51–55
support group for, 59, 159

Buses. *See* Transportation, public

Cameras, 141

Camping. *See* Travel

Cars, 139

Cerebral palsy, 3, 28, 29, 43, 53, 158

Children, concerns about having, 30–31

Chores, division of, 52, 56

Communication devices, 76, 124, 140–41, 153–54

Communication difficulties, 75–78, 90, 124, 153–54. *See also* Assertiveness; Telecommunications

Computers. *See* Adaptive equipment

Concentration, difficulties with, 22

Counselors, 23, 110

Crutches, 122, 136, 139

Dating, 25–28, 31–33

DCAT, 144

Depression, 22–23, 109. *See also* Emotions

Diet, 147

Disabilities
advantages vs. disadvantages of, 54
attitude toward one's own, 14–15
dealing with limitations of, 99–102
frustrations of having, 17–19
hereditary, 31
public attitudes toward, 36–37
separating self from one's, 11
sources for information on, 156–58

Discrimination, laws against. *See* Laws, disability

Doctors
developing relationship with, 146–47
selecting, 146

Dogs, support, 65, 108, 156